Practical Scala DSLs

Real-World Applications Using Domain Specific Languages

Pierluigi Riti

Apress®

Practical Scala DSLs: Real-World Applications Using Domain Specific Languages

Pierluigi Riti
Mullingar, Westmeath, Ireland

ISBN-13 (pbk): 978-1-4842-3035-0   ISBN-13 (electronic): 978-1-4842-3036-7
https://doi.org/10.1007/978-1-4842-3036-7

Library of Congress Control Number: 2017962308

Cover image by Freepik (www.freepik.com)

Managing Director: Welmoed Spahr
Editorial Director: Todd Green
Acquisitions Editor: Steve Anglin
Development Editor: Matthew Moodie
Technical Reviewer: Rohan Walia
Coordinating Editor: Mark Powers
Copy Editor: Michael G. Laraque

Distributed to the book trade worldwide by Springer Science+Business Media New York, 233 Spring Street, 6th Floor, New York, NY 10013. Phone 1-800-SPRINGER, fax (201) 348-4505, e-mail orders-ny@springer-sbm.com, or visit www.springeronline.com. Apress Media, LLC is a California LLC and the sole member (owner) is Springer Science+Business Media Finance Inc (SSBM Finance Inc). SSBM Finance Inc is a **Delaware** corporation.

For information on translations, please e-mail rights@apress.com, or visit http://www.apress.com/rights-permissions.

Apress titles may be purchased in bulk for academic, corporate, or promotional use. eBook versions and licenses are also available for most titles. For more information, reference our Print and eBook Bulk Sales web page at www.apress.com/bulk-sales.

Any source code or other supplementary material referenced by the author in this book is available to readers on GitHub via the book's product page, located at www.apress.com/9781484230350. For more detailed information, please visit www.apress.com/source-code.

Printed on acid-free paper

To my wife, Mara Ester, who brought me the best gift any man could receive: my two children, Nicole and Mattia. I love you.

Table of Contents

About the Author

Pierluigi Riti has more than 20 years of extensive experience in the design and development of different scale applications, particularly in the telecommunications and financial industries. At present, he is a senior DevOps engineer for a gaming company. He has expansive development skills that encompass the latest technologies, including Java, J2EE, C#, F#, .NET, Spring .NET, EF, WPF, WF, WinForm, WebAPI, MVC, Nunit, Scala, Spring, JSP, EJB, Struts, Struts2, SOAP, REST, C, C++, Hibernate, NHibernate, Weblogic, XML, XSLT, Unix script, Ruby, and Python.

Pierluigi loves to read about technology and architecture. When he isn't working, he enjoys spending time with his family.

About the Technical Reviewer

Rohan Walia is a software consultant with extensive experience in client-server, web-based, and enterprise application development. He is an Oracle Certified ADF Implementation Specialist and Sun Certified Java Programmer. He is responsible for designing and developing end-to-end Java/J2EE applications consisting of various cutting-edge frameworks and utilities. His areas of expertise include Oracle ADF, WebCenter, Spring, Hibernate, and Java/J2EE. When not working, Rohan loves to play tennis, travel, and hike. Rohan would like to thank his wife, Deepika Walia, for helping him to review this book.

Introduction

Hello, and welcome *to Practical Scala DSLs*. Scala has become very popular, and with more companies adopting the language every day, its popularity and growth have swelled.

DSLs, a way for designing software using its inherent techniques, is essentially a set of patterns that can describe software in "plain English." This book does not attempt to cover all the theory behind DSLs. A fantastic book, *Domain-Specific Languages*, by Martin Fowler (Addison-Wesley Professional, 2010) provides a basic understanding of this.

With this book, I wish to describe how to use DSLs in everyday projects. The scope of the book is to give the reader an idea of how to use a DSL on the job and, by the end of the book, see how DSLs can be used in different projects. What I intend to show is how to approach DSLs from a practical standpoint and teach the reader how to think about integrating DSLs in their daily work life.

To better understand the book, the reader must be familiar with Scala, able to write a simple program in Scala, and have an idea about its architecture. Ideally, the reader will have in addition some familiarity with Java programming. This is because both Scala and Java use the Java virtual machine (JVM), and some examples discussed in the text highlight the differences between Scala and Java. Last, the reader should have an affinity for an editor. I use IntelliJ, but any editor would be fine.

CHAPTER 1

Introduction to Scala

Scala has grown in popularity in the last years. Some describe the Scala language as the new "golden boy" of programming languages. More large companies have begun to adopt Scala for their core business needs, thus improving the popularity of the language and, of course, the market for it.

The popularity of the language is connected to the nature of the language itself. Scala borrows more of its syntax from other popular languages. For example, the method is declared like C but with optional braces.

At first glance, Scala looks like a dynamic language, such as Ruby or Python, but it is a strong static-type language, with all the advantages of this type.

Adding to all this, Scala has such features as for statement expressions, infix/suffix, and local type inference notation.

The nature of the language is perfect for domain specific languages (DSLs). Scala combines functional programming with object-oriented programming. Therefore, with Scala, when we must create a DSL, we can rely on a functional language to help us to develop an immutable function. On the one hand, this helps to ensure consistent results. On the other, most of the patterns used to create a DSL employ an object-oriented paradigm, which means that with Scala, we can also have the paradigm for creating the DSL.

In this chapter, I provide a brief introduction to the Scala language and highlight the main features of the language. The rest of the book is devoted to improving the reader's knowledge of the language, to create some DSL projects.

© Pierluigi Riti 2018

P. Riti, *Practical Scala DSLs*, https://doi.org/10.1007/978-1-4842-3036-7_1

I suggest using the REPL (Read-Evaluate-Print Loop) for use in the sample code for this chapter, because it provides immediate feedback about the operation we want to execute.

Note   Since Scala 2.11, the syntax to exit from the REPL has changed. If you have used the command exit() previously, you will realize that this command is no longer valid. Now, to exit, users must employ the sys.exit() command.

Basic Syntax

Scala is basically a strongly typed language, this means that we can annotate types for the following:

- Variable and value

- Method and function argument

- Method and function return type

For many programmers, this is nothing new. Languages such as Java or C# use the same kind of syntax. The best way of seeing how to use the syntax is to "get your hands dirty." Therefore, open the REPL and try some basic Scala commands.

Note   Scala runs on a JVM, but a big difference with Java is how Scala de-allocates unused memory. Scala automatically frees memory when data is no longer used.

To open the REPL, go to the command line and insert the command Scala. This will open the Scala interpreter, as follows:

```
$ scala
Welcome to Scala 2.12.2 (Java HotSpot(TM) 64-Bit Server VM,
Java 1.8.0_131).
Type in expressions for evaluation. Or try :help.

scala>
```

At first glance, the REPL looks like the interpreter of the interpreted language, such as Ruby or Python, but there is a big difference. Scala is a compiled language, which means that the REPL compiles the code and executes first to present the result.

Start writing some code to see how Scala works, such as

```
scala> 2+2
res0: Int = 4
```

Now, we can see Scala execute the code and create a temporary variable to assign the result. However, because Scala is typed, it defines the type of variable, in this case Int.

In Scala, the operators +, -, etc., are a simple function. In this case, writing 2 + 2 is equal to having a method with the left operand. The REPL is very useful in learning Scala, because it provides immediate feedback regarding the operation.

Variable and Value in Scala

With Scala, we can define two kinds of variables:

- A mutable variable, which is created with the reserved word var

- An immutable value, created with the reserved word val

This is probably the biggest difference from other languages. In Scala, it is high advisable to use the immutable variable val, because this doesn't break the rule of functional programming. I will discuss this rule later in the chapter.

The syntax for creating a variable or a value is the same: <kind> <name> : <type> = <value>. Now try the variable with the REPL and note the difference between a mutable and immutable variable. The first type of variable we declare is the mutable variable, declared with var.

```scala
scala> var num:Int = 4
num: Int = 4
scala> num = 8
num: Int = 8
```

Here, as you can see, we create a variable and assign the value of the variable. In this case, we define the type of the variable. We can change the value simply by calling the variable and assigning the new value. There is no difference in how this is done in other languages.

```scala
scala> num * 2
res0: Int = 8

scala> res0 + 2
res1: Int = 10
```

The statement that follows is perfectly valid. In the event that we have not assigned the name of the variable, Scala creates a temporary variable and associates the result with this variable. In this way, we can easily use the temporary variable to execute some other operations. Try to see now how an immutable variable works.

```scala
scala> val new_num = 4
new_num: Int = 4
scala> new_num = 8
<console>:12: error: reassignment to val
       new_num = 8
```

In this case, we created a variable new_num, but we haven't explicitly specified a type. Scala inspects and assigns the correct type. The process for creating the val is exactly the same as for creating a var. The only difference is that if we try to reassign the value, we obtain an error. For many developers, it can be strange to use an immutable variable instead of a mutable variable, but if you look at your code, you can see how simple it is to replace the mutable variable with an immutable one.

Naming in Scala

Scala allows you to name a variable with any letter, number, or some special operator characters. According to the following from the Scala Language Specification, we learn how to define these operator characters:

> *...all other characters in \u0020-007F and Unicode categories Sm [Symbol/Math]...except parentheses ([]) and periods.*

Following are some rules for combining letters, numbers, and characters when naming identifiers in Scala:

- A letter followed by zero or more letters or digits, for example, var a, var AabcdA, var a1b

- A letter followed by zero or more digits, underscores (_), or letters, for example, var a_b or val a_ = 10

- An underscore (_) followed by zero or more letters or digits, for example, var _abcd_

First Example in Scala

Now try to write a simple bubble sort algorithm in Scala.

```scala
def bubbleSort(arr_input: Array[Int]): Array[Int] = {
  val size = arr_input.size - 1
  for (a <- 1 to size) {
```

```
  for (b <- size to a by -1) {
    if (arr_input(b) < arr_input(b - 1)) {
      val x = arr_input(b)
      arr_input(b) = arr_input(b - 1)
      arr_input(b - 1) = x
    }
  }
}
arr_input
}
```

This simple example shows some Scala functionality. First, we see how to use an immutable variable instead of a mutable one. Starting with this simple example, we can define the principal Scala syntax.

Define a Method and Function in Scala

The syntax for defining a function in Scala is similar to that of any other language. The structure is the following:

def function_name ([list of parameter]) : [return type]

In the previous example, we defined the method bubblesort:

def bubbleSort (arr_input: Array[Int]): Array[Int]

The list of the parameter can be any valid object of Scala or another function. This characteristic of Scala is called a higher-order function.

The higher-order function is a feature of a functional language such as Scala. For example, imagine that we want to define the function apply and use another function as a parameter.

def apply(internal: Int => String, value:Int) = internal(value)

The function apply takes a function internal as a parameter and applies the function internal to the other parameter, value.

The higher-order function highlights an interesting difference in how Scala defines a function. A function in Scala is an expression that takes a parameter and returns a value.

```
val addOne = (num:Int) => num +1
```

Of course, we can have a function without a parameter.

```
val fixValue = () => 9
val theAnswer=() => 42
```

The principal difference between functions and methods in Scala is that, this because a method requires a name, the anonymous function is used normally with the functional programming. An anonymous function is not a new concept to Java developers. In Java, when defining the interface, we usually define the event in the anonymous class.

Scala uses the anonymous class in a different way. In Scala, it is possible to define what is known as a *first-class function*. This function accepts another function for parameters. An anonymous function can be used, for example, to filter a list. The code for this would look like the following:

```
scala> val list = List.range(1, 20)
list: List[Int] = List(1, 2, 3, 4, 5, 6, 7, 8, 9, 10, 11, 12,
13, 14, 15, 16, 17, 18, 19)

scala> val evens = list.filter((num : Int) => num % 2 == 0)
evens: List[Int] = List(2, 4, 6, 8, 10, 12, 14, 16, 18)
```

In the preceding code, we create an anonymous function to create the value of the variable evens: list.filter((num : Int) => num % 2 == 0). Here you can see that we used an anonymous function for the parameter of another function.

Classes in Scala

In Scala, a class is defined with this syntax:

```
class nameOfTheClass([list of parameters]){ body of the class }
```

The class is the core of object-oriented programming. For
experimenting with classes, it is best to open the REPL and try to create a
simple Scala class.

```
scala> class TheQuestion()
defined class TheQuestion
```

The following code shows the basic class in Scala. From what you can
see, it is not mandatory for a class to have a body. Of course, a body is not
really useful for a class such as that in the sample code, but the simple class
used helps us to understand some functionality of the class. For creating
an instance of a class, we must use the word new.

```
scala> val question = new TheQuestion()
question: TheQuestion = TheQuestion@1726750
```

Now it is possible to see that a class has been created for the name
and a hexadecimal number. This number is the JVM value associated
with the class. A class such as that is not very useful, but it does have all
the properties of a simple class. In the REPL, start to call the name of the
variable and then press tab. In this case, Scala shows all the commands
that can be used for the class.

```
scala> question.
!=          ->
ensuring    formatted    isInstanceOf    notifyAll       wait

##          ==           eq              getClass        ne
synchronized    ?

+    asInstanceOf    equals    hashCode    notify        toString
```

8

This code creates a class instance and associates it with a variable. Try now to create a simple class in Scala.

```scala
class TheQuestion(){
  def theAnswer():Int = {
    return 42
  }
}
```

The preceding code shows how to create a simple class in Scala. Inside the body of the class, we can define the method exposed by the class. This method defines the operation executed by the class.

To create an instance of the class that uses this, we can employ the following syntax:

```scala
scala> val question= new TheQuestion()
question: TheQuestion = TheQuestion@e5d3e1
```

To use the method, we can simply use the dot notation, as in other languages.

```scala
scala> question.theAnswer
res1: Int = 42
```

Singleton Object

Scala differs from other languages in how it creates a singleton object. For creating a singleton object, the syntax is similar to what we use for creating a class, but we substitute the word `class` with `object`.

```scala
object TheQuestion {
  def main(args: Array[String]): Unit ={
    val theAnswer:Int = 42
    println(theAnswer)
  }
}
```

You can see that the definition is similar to a simple class. In this case, we have created a `main` method for use in the object. Because this is a singleton, we don't require the word `new` in order to create it. The syntax for creating the instance is like the following:

```
scala> val answer = TheQuestion.main(null)
42
answer: Unit = ()
```

The singleton object follows the same rules as other languages. In this case, however, because the method `main` has an array as a parameter, we use the word `null` to create a null object.

Types in Scala

In Scala, as in any other language, we can find two kinds of types: *numerical*, such as `Int` or `Double`, and *non-numerical* types, such as `char` and `string`.

The difference between Scala and other languages with regard to types is principally one: in Scala, there is no primitive type. This means that any type in Scala is an object. For example, when we define an `Int`, we create an instance of an object `Integer`.

Converting Numeric Types

Scala can automatically convert numeric types from one to another. This can occur only in one direction: from a shorter type to a longer type. Table 1-1 shows the numeric type ranked from the lowest to the highest. Numeric types make it possible, for example, to convert a byte into any other type listed. Note, however, that a `Double` cannot be converted into any other type.

Table 1-1. *Numerical Data Type in Scala*

Name	Definition	Size
Byte	Signed integer	1 byte
Short	Signed integer	2 bytes
Integer	Signed integer	4 bytes
Long	Signed integer	8 bytes
Float	Signed floating point	4 bytes
Double	Signed floating point	8 bytes

String in Scala

A string in Scala is based on the same kind of string in the JVM. Scala adds some unique features, such as multiline and interpolation.

For creating a `String` in Scala, we can use double quotes. Inside the double quotes we can write our string.

```
scala> val theGuide = "don't panic"
theGuide: String = don't panic
```

From the previous example, you can see that a string is very easy to create. You can create a string with special characters using the backslash (\).

```
scala> val theQuestion= "the Answer to the Ultimate Question of
life, \nthe Universe,\nand Everything"

theQuestion: String =
the Answer to the Ultimate Question of life,
the Universe,
and Everything
```

In this case, Scala creates the string with a new line character. This creates the string in multiple lines. It is possible to concatenate the string with the plus sign (+), as follows:

```
scala> val sayHello = "Hello"+" reader"
sayHello: String = Hello reader
```

In this case, we can see Scala concatenate the string into one single string. It is possible to compare the equality of a string by using the operator ==. Scala differs from Java in that in Scala, we don't check the equality of the object but the equality of the string values, as follows:

```
scala> val string_compare_1 = "String 1"
string_compare_1: String = String 1

scala> val string_compare_2 = "String 1"
string_compare_2: String = String 1

scala> val compare = string_compare_1==string_compare_2
compare: Boolean = true
```

We can see that the two strings have the same value, which, in Scala, are the same. If we try to compare the strings, the value true is returned.

Multiline String

To create a multiline string in Scala, we use three double quotes after the start of a string.

```
scala> val theFinalAnswer = """ Six by nine. Forty-two.
     | That's it. That's all there is.
     | I always thought something was fundamentally wrong with
       the universe """

theFinalAnswer: String =
" Six by nine. Forty-two.
```

That's it. That's all there is.
I always thought something was fundamentally wrong with the
universe"

Multiline strings follow the same rules as other strings. This means that
we can use special characters and comparisons as in a normal string.

A multistring is very useful when we want to add specifically formatted
string in a code. For example, if we want to have a JSON string in the code,
to prepare a return for an output or simply for a test, we can write the string
as follows:

```
scala> val jsonString: String =
     |    """
     |    |{
     |    |"name":"PracticalScalaDSL",
     |    |"author":"Pierluigi Riti",
     |    |"publisher":"Apress"
     |    |}
     |    """
jsonString: String =
"
{
"name":"PracticalScalaDSL",
"author":"Pierluigi Riti",
"publisher":"Apress"
}
    "
```

String Interpolation

In Scala, it is easy to concatenate a string by using the plus sign (+),
but there is a niftier way of doing this: *string interpolation*. With this
interpolation, Scala replaces the variable with the string value. To use a
variable to interpolate a string, the dollar sign ($) is used.

```
scala> val hello = "world"
hello: String = world
scala> println(s"Hello $hello")
Hello world
```

We can see from the preceding sample code that we can create a variable and then substitute it when we print out the string. This technique allows us to maintain clear and compact code that is easy to read and, of course, maintain. We can interpolate a string when assigning another variable too. In this case, we must use the syntax ${<variable name>}.

```
scala> val sayHello= s"Hello ${hello}"
sayHello: String = Hello world
```

To use the interpolation, we must use the char s, which tells Scala to create a string with the variable we write, and Scala then interpolates the string with the variable.

Note   From a memory perspective, it is better to interpolate a string, because a string, as a JVM/Java object, is immutable. This means that when we use the plus sign (+) to create a string, we create three string objects when we concatenate only two strings. This is because, first, Scala allocates memory to the first string, then the second string, and, finally, the third string, as a concatenation of the previous strings. When we interpolate, we have only two strings, because the second is created based on the substitution of the variable.

Expressions in Scala

Scala is a functional language and, as such, functional programming was the primary intent of the inventor of the language. Given this context, I want to describe what an *expression* means in Scala.

An expression in Scala is a single line of code that returns a value. This is very important for reducing *side effects,* because they always have the same response to an operation. The scope of functional programming is to define the function in a mathematical way. This means that every function must always return the same value, if it is always sent the same parameter.

This occurs because the function is essentially immutable and isn't influenced by changes occurring outside the function. This is done to reduce or further eliminate side effects. Side effects are essentially the result of a change to a variable or an expression that changes a value. When the variable outside changes, this violates the functional programming itself.

We can define different types of expressions in Scala:

- A simple string, Int, or any other

- A variable

- A value

- A function

An expression is very useful for moving from object-oriented programming to functional programming. Expressions are used in everyday programming, but you may not have been aware of this. For example, the syntax

```
var variable:String = "value"
```

defines an expression. Using a variable, of course, we can use the same syntax to define a value, as follows:

```
val variable:String = "value"
```

In the preceding, an expression has been created with a function, but suppose, for example, you want to define a function for calculating the area of a square.

```
val square=(x: Int) => x*x
```

The preceding code indicates how to use a function to create an expression.

Conditional Expression

The conditional expression if..else is the core construction of all programming languages. Scala uses the same logical base of other languages for the if..else conditional expression.

The syntax of the if..else is

```
if(<Boolean>) <expression>
```

If the Boolean condition is True, expression executes.

```
scala> if (10 % 3 > 0) println("Not a multiple")
Not a multiple
```

In this example, we use an expression for checking the Boolean value. If 10 is not divisible by 3 it prints "Not a Multiple", so we can see the use of an if..else in Scala is the same of other languages.

In case we want to define an else condition, we can use this syntax:

```
if(boolean) expression   else expression
```

We can now write a more complex if..else condition:

```
scala> if (10 % 2 > 0) println("Not a multiple") else
("Multiple")
res2: Any = Multiple
```

Pattern Matching Expression

Scala doesn't have a switch command like Java or C#. In Scala, we have the command match, which is more flexible than switch.

The syntax for the pattern matching is:

```
<expression> match{
        Case <pattern match> => <expression>
}
```

The pattern match can be a value or a regular expression; for example, a simple pattern matching can be

```
scala> val number1 = 10
number1: Int = 10

scala> val number2 = 20
number2: Int = 20

scala> val max = number1 > number2 match{
     | case true => number1
     | case false => number2
     | }
max: Int = 20
```

Here we can see that we have created two values and that the expression is essentially a simple check of these two values. When we identify the bigger, we write out the number.

Multiple Conditions

You can use more conditions in pattern matching. For example, it is possible to check the month of the year to correspond with the season.

```
val month = "JAN"

val season = month match{
  case "DEC" | "JAN" | "FEB" =>
    "Winter"
```

```scala
  case "MAR" | "APR" | "MAY" =>
    "Spring"
  case "JUN" | "JUL" | "AUG" =>
    "Summer"
  case "SEP" | "OCT" | "NOV" =>
    "Autumn"
}
```

In this case, we match a string using an "or" and can see that the pattern matching is similar but more powerful than with the switch structure. My suggestion is to play with this pattern to learn best what you can do with pattern matching. We can, of course, use a wildcard to parse the case not actually present.

```scala
val month = "JAN"

val season = month match{
  case "DEC" | "JAN" | "FEB" =>
    "Winter"
  case "MAR" | "APR" | "MAY" =>
    "Spring"
  case "JUN" | "JUL" | "AUG" =>
    "Summer"
  case "SEP" | "OCT" | "NOV" =>
    "Autumn"
  case _ =>
    "Not a month"
}
```

In this case, the code shows the result "Not a month". Of course, it is possible to specify the type of variable we want to use for the pattern matching. Here, we need to define the kind of variable following the case. An example can be if we want to check a value, based on a specific type.

```
Val theAnswer:Int = 42

val anyAnswer:Any = theAnswer

anyAnswer match {
  case theAnswer:String => "String Value"
  case theAnswer:Int => "Integer Value"
  case theAnswer:Double => "Double Value"
}
```

With this simple example, we create a variable, and, after, we assign this variable to a type Any. This kind of variable is the highest in numeric value, and this means that it is possibly associated with any other kind of variable. In the example, we try to check with the pattern matching to Identify which kind of value is associated with the variable of the kind Any.

Pattern Guard

A *pattern guard* is an if expression to check a Boolean condition used for executing the pattern matching. This is useful, for example, when we want to check if a string or object is not null.

```
val empyString:String = null

val empStr = empyString match{
  case sea if sea!= null =>
    println(s"Received '$sea'")
  case sea =>
    println(s"Received a null value")
}
```

Range and Loop

A for loop in Scala executes a block of code for a certain number of executions. For example, we can use a loop when we want to iterate all elements of an array.

```scala
val myArray:Array[String] = new Array[String](10)

for (i <- 0 until myArray.length){
  print(s"element of the array $myArray(i)")
}
```

In this example, we create an array of an empty element string. The code initializes all elements to the default value, in the case of string, null. We then use the length of the array to identify the number of the iteration. In Scala, it is possible to use the object Range to create a maximum number of the element.

To create a Range object in Scala, we use the following syntax:

```
<start integer> to or until <end integer> <increment>
```

The increment is optional, but if it is not, specify it as 1. Imagine now that we want to create a for loop to show some numbers, as follows:

```scala
scala> for (number <- 1 to 12) { println(s"Month $number") }
Month 1
Month 2
Month 3
Month 4
Month 5
Month 6
Month 7
Month 8
Month 9
```

```
Month 10
Month 11
Month 12
```

In this case, we count from 1 to 12 and show out a string with the string month and number. We can specify different increments using the word by.

```
scala> for (number <- 1 to 12 by 2) { println(s"Month $number")
}
Month 1
Month 3
Month 5
Month 7
Month 9
Month 11
```

In this case, we see the number is incremented by 2, and this reduces the number of elements generated by the range object. In Scala, it is possible to create a range from a List or Array easily. By using the method toList or toArray, Scala converts the object range directly to a List or an Array. It is preferable to use a List in Scala instead of an array, because a List is an immutable structure. This means that when we create a List, we can't modify it. The List does not allow side effects, and it is important in functional programming to avoid these.

```
scala> val day_of_week = (1 to 7).toArray
day_of_week: Array[Int] = Array(1, 2, 3, 4, 5, 6, 7)

scala> val day_of_week = (1 to 7).toList
day_of_week: List[Int] = List(1, 2, 3, 4, 5, 6, 7)
```

Note   It is possible to omit the parentheses, but in that case, you must use postfixOps. The faster way of doing this is to import the class postfixOps, as follows:

```scala
scala> import scala.language.postfixOps
import scala.language.postfixOps
scala> val day_of_week = 1 to 7 toList

day_of_week: List[Int] = List(1, 2, 3, 4, 5, 6, 7)
```

It is possible to use the word yield to create an IndexSeq object. This object translated the value of the result in a Vector, as follows:

```scala
scala> val day_of_week = for (x <- 1 to 7) yield {s"$x"}
day_of_week: scala.collection.immutable.IndexedSeq[String] =
Vector(1, 2, 3, 4,5, 6, 7)
```

It is possible to use an *iterator guard* to execute the increment only in certain conditions. An iterator guard is an if condition for verifying whether to execute the increment first.

```scala
scala> val even = for(i <- 1 to 20 if i%2 == 0) yield i
odds: scala.collection.immutable.IndexedSeq[Int] = Vector(2, 4,
6, 8, 10, 12, 14, 16, 18, 20)
```

Other Loops

In Scala, it is possible to create a loop not only by using the for syntax but by using the while and do..while loops. These loops repeat a statement until a Boolean is false.

```scala
var count = 10

while(count > 0){
  println(count)
  count -=1
```

```
}
10
9
8
7
6
5
4
3
2
1
```

The while syntax is very simple: the condition of execution is checked *after* the loop. For example, when the value of the variable count is 0, the code is executed. Only when the variable is -1, does the loop stop.

The do..while loop is similar to the while loop. The difference is that the variable is checked *before* the execution of the loop.

```scala
scala> var count = 10
count: Int = 10
scala> do{
     |    println(count)
     |    count -=1
     | }while(count >0 )
10
9
8
7
6
5
4
3
2
1
```

We can see that the result is exactly the same. The only difference is that the conditional expression is checked first, to call the new loop. This saves a computational execution and occurs because the do..while loop checks the value after the statement. In this case, when the variable reaches 0, the process is stopped.

Data Structures

Until now, I have presented only the basic syntax for the language, but a real program must memorize the data in the data structure in order to manipulate it. I will now discuss the different data structures we can use in Scala.

In Scala there are six basic data structures, as follows:

- Array
- List
- Set
- Tuple
- Map

In the next sections, I will attempt to identify the principal differences between these data structures.

Array

An array is a mutable collection and preserves the order of the element we insert. The data in the array is all the same type. The data is not sorted in order, which means that if we create an array with the value (2,1,3), the element of the array remains in that order. An array can also contain duplicated values.

```
scala> val myArray:Array[String] = new Array[String](10)
myArray: Array[String] = Array(null, null, null, null, null,
null, null, null, null, null)
```

In the preceding code, an empty array is defined for a string of ten elements. Because we haven't specified the value, Scala fills the array with the default value of a string, in this case, the value null.

We can access an array for reading/modifying a value on the array, by using the index of the array. Say, for example, that we want to change the value of the first element of the array. The code would look like the following:

```
scala> myArray(0) = "test"
scala> myArray
res7: Array[String] = Array(test, null, null, null, null, null,
null, null, null, null)
```

Is possible to create an array by just defining the elements of the array itself.

```
scala> val myArray_new = Array(1,2,3,4,5,6,5)
myArray_new: Array[Int] = Array(1, 2, 3, 4, 5, 6, 5)
```

List

A list is an immutable collection. A list preserves the order of the element we insert in it and, like an array, stores only data of the same type, although it can have a duplicated value.

```
scala> val myList = List("a","b","c","b")
myList: List[String] = List(a, b, c, b)
```

A list is an immutable collection, which means that it is not possible to update the value. In fact, it is not possible to create a list with a default value. If we try to update a value on a list, Scala returns an exception.

```
scala> myList(3) = 10
<console>:13: error: value update is not a member of
List[String]
        myList(3) = 10
```

Set

A set is an unordered immutable sequence. A set doesn't preserve the order of the element, and it is not possible to add a duplicate element to the set. If we add duplicate elements, the duplicates are deleted by the set itself.

```
scala> val numbers = Set(1,2,3,4,4,5,3,3,2,1)
numbers: scala.collection.immutable.Set[Int] =
Set(5, 1, 2, 3, 4)
```

Tuple

A tuple is a simple logical collection of data. We can store data, like, for example, user data, without having to define a class.

```
scala> val servers=("localhost", 80)
servers: (String, Int) = (localhost,80)
```

It is possible to access to the element of a tuple by using the positional index. Tuple is a 1-based container.

```
scala> servers._1
res0: String = localhost
```

Tuple can be used with pattern matching as a condition for case. If we must create a tuple of only two elements, we can use the sugar syntax ->, as follows:

```
scala> 1 -> 2
res1: (Int, Int) = (1,2)
```

Following is how, in a tuple, we can add more than two elements:

```
scala> val users=("Pierluigi","Riti",15,9,1975)
users: (String, String, Int, Int, Int) = (Pierluigi,Riti,
15,9,1975)
```

Map

A map is an iterable, immutable collection of key/value pair. To create a map, we use the syntax used for creating the tuple. Every tuple is a key/value pair:

```
scala> Map("one" -> 1, "two" -> 2)
res1: scala.collection.immutable.Map[String,Int] = Map(one ->
1, two -> 2)
```

It is possible to associate another map to a key.

```
scala> Map("one" ->Map("one" ->1))
res2: scala.collection.immutable.Map[String,scala.collection.
immutable.Map[String,Int]] = Map(one -> Map(one -> 1))
```

Summary

In this chapter, I introduced the basic syntax of Scala. I explained the basic Scala syntax without delving into it deeply but only to provide an understanding of how to use Scala. In the next chapter, we will dive deeper into these basic concepts, and I will introduce other Scala concepts related to design and implementation of DSLs. As I suggested, the best way to learn Scala and unleash the potential of this language is to get your hands dirty with the REPL.

CHAPTER 2

Introduction to DSL

DSLs (domain specific languages) are everywhere. When, for example, we go for a pizza or a hamburger, we talk with a "specific" language to place our orders. A DSL is a language used in a specific *domain* to solve a problem.

A DSL is the opposite of a general-purpose language, such as, for example, English or Italian. When we use a DSL, we are using a general-purpose language (GPL). When we go to our coffee shop to order a beverage, we use a general-purpose language, English, to solve a domain problem—ordering—for example, a large, cold Frappuccino. A large, cold Frappuccino is essentially a DSL.

In this chapter, I will identify the key concepts of DSLs and provide some examples of existing DSLs.

Definition of DSL

A DSL is a computer language specialized for a specific domain. A DSL is essentially the opposite of a GPL. By GPL), I mean every language that can be used to develop something. For example, Java, C#, and Scala are all GPL languages. With a DSL, we want only to solve a specific domain problem, so we design the language specifically for the domain. A DSL can't be used outside of the domain, because it is not designed for flexibility.

© Pierluigi Riti 2018
P. Riti, *Practical Scala DSLs*, https://doi.org/10.1007/978-1-4842-3036-7_2

In IT, there are lots of DSLs. One example is Hypertext Markup Language (HTML). This language is valid only when we want to design a web page but is completely useless if, for example, we want to design a graphical interface.

We can identify two kinds of DSLs, *internal* (or *embedded*) and *external*. The difference between these two types is how they are created.

Difference Between Internal and External DSLs

An internal, or embedded, DSL is one that is created internally in a GPL, for example, when we create a set of classes with Java to solve a domain problem. Internal DSLs are very useful for creating an application program interface (API).

When we use an embedded DSL, we are using a subset of the GPL to create our language, and, therefore, we lose all the flexibility associated with the GPL). On the other hand, however, we can build software that is more readable by the domain expert. This means that the developer can solve an issue or change a functionality faster. For example, if we want to parse an Excel file, we can have a code like the following:

```
LoadFile("C:\file.xls")
        .read_column("A1")
        .read_column("A2")
        .save_CSV("file.csv")
```

This code essentially uses a DSL to read two columns from an Excel file and saves it in a comma-separated values (CSV) file. We can use any language to create this chain. In case we have to change the Excel column, we need only to create the chain with a different column value.

An *external* DSL is a kind of DSL that is not correlated with a language. CSS or a regular expression are good examples of external DSLs.

The difference in DSLs is not only in their definition but in how they are implemented. For example, when we create an external DSL, we must define a language and parse it. Conversely, when we create an internal DSL, we can create a *fluent API*. This means that we can define a specific pattern that can be called as well as a fluent interface. The term, coined by Eric Evans and Martin Fowler, reflects the fact that when we use this pattern, we are essentially creating APIs as readable as plain English.

We can use this pattern for our language, because it improves the readability of the code and helps to reach the goal of the DSL.

Designing a Good DSL

When we design a DSL, it doesn't matter if it's an internal DSL or an external DSL. We just have to follow some basic rules to achieve a good result.

- *Encapsulation*: A good DSL must hide the implementation details of the problem by exposing only what is necessary to solve the problem.

- *Efficiency*: Because the implementation details are hidden, the developer should have less work to do when changing the use of the DSL. Of course, to do that, the engineer responsible for the creation of the DSL must be careful to create the APIs in a good and simple way. To do that, extra care must be given to the design of the API and the DSL. Better API design translates into better use of the same and reduced work when, for example, a consumer requires an update. When a developer uses our DSL, the important thing is for it to have the same functionality. This means that when we have to change the API, for example, to improve new functionality, we must be careful not to break the actual functionality we have implemented. This can be done using the correct level of interface and design.

31

- *Communication*: Because the DSL is designed for fixing a specific domain problem, methods must be given a name that is understandable to the domain expert. This means, for a domain expert, that it's easier to identify a problem in the creation of the software.

Of course, creating a good DSL isn't easy. To respect all rules, we must write code that is well-documented and essentially self-explanatory when we configure, for example, the API for the internal DSL. We must be sure to have a good level of abstraction, and we must design a good API.

When we create the DSL, we must identify the domain of the problem and, based on that, define a common dictionary capable of solving the problem. What we have to do is define the *model domain*. In this way, it is easier to define a dictionary and share this dictionary with the developer. In DSLs, it is essentially the domain that drives the definition of the language. Some examples follow:

- RubyDSL, used in Puppet to define the manifest for the configuration

- SQL

- HTML

These languages are all essentially DSL languages, because they are specific to solving one problem and can't be used to create a general-purpose program.

Analyze the Domain

When designing DSLs, we must identify the model for the domain we have to use for work. Defining the model domain is the basis for defining a correct DSL. When we analyze the model domain, essentially, we identify all entities and relations connected to the domain. When we have designed and identified the correct entity domain, we can start to define a common dictionary for our DSL. A common dictionary is necessary to improve the communication and, of course, gain one of the pillars for designing a good DSL. The *problem domain* is the process whereby we identify *entities* and *constraints*. Identifying these is an exercise we must perform to better understand a problem with the domain. When we do this exercise, we figure out the *common language* of the domain, that is, the language we must use for communicating with the expert of the domain.

When we have identified the problem domain, we can define the solution domain. The solution domain provides all the tools we can use to solve the problem. After the problem is identified and the solution domain established, we can start to model the domain.

Imagine, for example, that we want to identify and model a continuous integration system. First, we must identify all the entities and, after that, begin to design our system (see Figure 2-1).

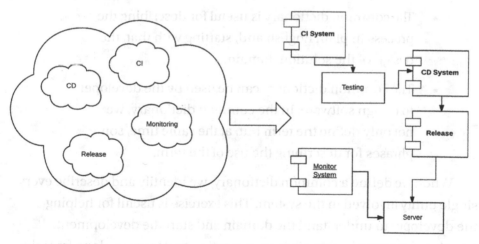

Figure 2-1. *Translating the problem domain into a solution domain*

When we identify the problem domain, we can design the solution domain. The solution domain is the architecture of the system. Here, we identify the major components we must implement to solve the problem. Based on this, we can design a common dictionary for defining a common language for the DSL.

Creating a Common Dictionary

When we design the solution domain, we essentially identify all entities involved in the DSL. The common dictionary is important for identifying the language used to talk about the system, like when we go to our favorite coffee shop and ask for a cold frappuccino. This is necessary for a mutual understanding of the problem by an engineer and businesspeople. This is also important for improving the quality of the communication and the quality of the system. It is possible to identify some advantages related to the creation of the common dictionary.

- The common dictionary can be easily used for testing and is the basis for describing the test plan. Based on that, we can easily identify the process of the software.

- The common dictionary is useful for describing the process in plain English and, starting with that, the design of the solution domain.

- The common dictionary can be used by the developer to design software. In the common dictionary, we not only define the term but, at the same time, some phrases for describing the use of the term.

When we define a common dictionary, we identify and describe every single entity involved in the system. This exercise is useful for helping the developer to understand the domain and start the development. Imagine, for example, describing some action that must be done from the Continuous Integration (CI) system we want to define. The phrase might be: "The Continuous Integration system must connect on Git, download the source code for a specific language, and compile it."

When we define this phrase, we essentially use a common dictionary and create a use case for the software, starting to design our DSL for solving the problem.

Sample DSLs

Imagine now that we want to write a simple code sample of the DSL to describe a Continuous Integration) system. The code would look like the following:

```scala
object ContinousIntegration {
  object Connect { def git = (x: source.type) => x }
  object source { def control = (x: language.type) => x }
  object language { def kind = (x: language.type ) => x}
  object compile { def scala = (x: language.type ) => x }
  implicit def string(s : String) : language.type = language

  def main(args: Array[String]): Unit = {
    Connect git source control language kind "Scala"
  }
}
```

In this brief short example, a functionality for Continuous Integration) is described. We have essentially created a set object, then used this object to write a phrase that we can read in plain English. In this case, we write "**Connect Git source control language kind "Scala"**." This is essentially the business functionality, and it makes it easy to understand whether we've made a mistake.

Scala is fantastic for this, and writing code in this way gives users very clear and compact code that is simple to read and maintain.

Note   In Scala, the "dot notation" is not mandatory. In the preceding code, we call the function without using the dot to call the method. This allows the developer to create code that can be read like plain English.

In the case of a business, an expert can easily read the code we wrote and tell where there is an error. In case, there is—in the business logic. This is the true power of a DSL. By allowing a business to understand the code, communication between the business and engineering teams is greatly improved.

In this case, we have created an *internal DSL*. This is because we used a GPL), Scala, to define a specific subset of the language, in this case, a representation of a CI process. We can see that we wrote an internal DSL to match the defined use case story. This is the real power of the DSL. We can easily create a bond between the user story and the language we develop, which allows everyone to validate our story from the start, with the test case. This reduces bugs and improves the quality of the software.

DSL Goals

When you create a DSL language, you must have a clear objective in your mind. The DSLs should be understandable and verifiable to the business user. To design a good DSL, some specific rules must be followed.

- DSLs design a "language." This means that the user doesn't have to know the details about the implementation. The developer only needs to use the common dictionary to define the business and then shift the focus to the correct implementation of the method.

- DSLs define a very small language. We define restricted sets of words that we can use to implement the solution for the business domain. Because of this, it is possible for a developer to learn the terms easily and improve his/her knowledge.

- DSLs are born of the idea of mapping a business domain in a common language. To allow this, we define a common dictionary, in which we define the word and the functionality, after the developer translates the word into a function. Imagine, for example, that we want to create a DSL for a financial application. We have a specific term to define. This is because the developer doesn't have knowledge of, for example, the terms *bid* or *ask*, or any other financial term. Creating the common dictionary helps to define the term and, therefore, the developer, to understand the scope of the DSL.

Realizing all three of the preceding goals in designing a DSL requires that the software we design with also be of good quality. Today, there is a great variety of languages, and some, like Scala, allow developers to write very good DSLs.

When we want to implement a DSL for our project, we start from day zero of the project. In terms of the software and solution architecture, this means that we begin to design the software by adhering to the following rules: the function should be internally well-documented and, at the same time, the name should be a valid name for the business. A correct DSL implementation uses some defined architectural pattern. For example, in Martin Fowler's *Domain-Specific Languages,* it is possible to find a good description of all the patterns that can be used for design and implementation of our DSL.

Another big benefit associated with the use of DSLs is removal of the communication barriers between a business user and developer. When we design and implement a DSL, a developer must understand the business domain. For this reason, we define a common dictionary, but the exercise connected with the "design" of the common dictionary improves the business knowledge of the developer. We use DSL languages nearly every day, but without realizing this. Some common DSL languages are

- SQL
- RSpec
- Cucumber
- SBT
- ANT
- HTML
- CSS
- ANTLR

These languages represent only a fraction of DSLs. Everyone has likely used one of these languages at one time or another in their lives without being aware of it. All these languages, however, are designed to solve a specific business domain issue.

Implementing a DSL

We now move on to how we can implement a DSL. Until now, I presented only the processes that we can follow to design a DSL. Our focus can now shift to what we can do, from a developer's point of view, to implement the language.

The first decision we must make is how to structure the language. This means that, first, we must decide whether we want to use an internal or external DSL. This is not an easy decision, because using one or the other technique drives the architecture definition and essentially defines how the developer and the business transform the business solution into a software.

To define the DSL, the first decisions we must make are to

- Define the grammar of the language for both kinds of DSLs (internal and external) and define a specific grammar for defining the business. This means that we must define a complete grammar for creating the "language."

- Create the parser necessary for defining the semantic model of the language. When we have the grammar, we must also create the parser, to "translate" the language into the software.

How to implement these steps defines the difference between an external and internal DSL. A common point among DSLs is their grammar. The differences occur when we have to parse the DSLs. In the case of internal DSLs, essentially for parsing the grammar, we define some API, using, for example, the *Expression Builder* pattern, for creating our final phrase. For an external DSL, the parser normally reads the text, from an external file, for example, parsing all files and then creating the call for the proper API, to meet the business requirements.

In the end, both techniques solve the same problem. The only difference is how to parse the grammar. For an internal DSL, the grammar is solved using a set of the call to an internal API The sequence of the call for the API defines the business requirements and, in the end, achieves the business requirements.

One example of a fluent API for parsing a grammar is JMock. In JMock, for example, we can write something like the following:

```
mock.expects(once()).method("my_method").with(or(stringContains
("hello"),stringContains("howyourday")) );
```

This code essentially parses a grammar, in this case, the method for checking if the name of the method contains the word we have to test.

In the case of an external DSL, for example, we use the grammar for creating an external file. This file is called by the program and put in a three-part syntax. When we have the three parts, we start to call the API and use the results to define an action or call another API.

Grammar and Data Parsing

When we define the DSL, one of the most important aspects of this is the *grammar*. The grammar is retrieved from the common dictionary and should be used to define the business solution.

By the term *grammar*, we are referring to a set of rules that we can use to stream text and turn it into software. Every developer uses a grammar every day. For example, when creating a variable in Scala, we use a specific grammar. Imagine, for example, that we want to define a new grammar for executing a sum of two numbers. The syntax might be `sum:= number '+' number`. This would tell us how to execute an operation, and in case we found the expression *2 + 2*, this would be valid for the system. The grammar doesn't tell us how we must resolve the expression, only that the expression is valid.

Who tells us what kind of operation to execute provides the context. For example, we can define a two-sum operation, one by a number, the other by a string. In the case of a number, we can execute the sum, so that the operation 2 + 2 returns 4. In the case of two strings, the result of 2 + 2 is 22. The context of the operation is driven by the *semantics* of the operation we want to define. In the previous example, we used a number or string.

After we have defined the grammar for the language, the other important step involves *parsing the data*. The parser must read the language, using the grammar we have defined and according to how we have instructed this grammar to be used. This step is crucial for the efficiency of the DSL. When we parse the data, we probably have to store more information in memory. To speed the process, we can create a *symbolic table*. This is nothing more than a dictionary. The key is the grammar word we require to parse, for example, the +, and the value that is the object of the operation we must call with the parameter. The symbolic table is the core of our parser. This keeps in the memory all words and functions, thus helping the developer to translate the language into code. The parser uses the symbolic table for creating the call function that translates the syntax into code.

First DSL Implementation

Until now, the discussion has centered more on the theory behind DSLs. Now I present a very short piece of code to show what a DSL looks like. It's time now to present some examples of real implementation, to see how to create an actual DSL.

The first step in defining a DSL is to design the common dictionary. Let's see now how to define a common dictionary. I will use the example of a CI) system (see Table 2-1).

Table 2-1. *A Sample Common Dictionary*

Word	Definition
Repository	A place where software is stored. To connect to the repository, we must know the URL, the user, and the password. We can specify the kind of repository, for example, Git. Every repository can have a different parameter.
Compile	To build a specific software language, when we compile, we must define the language to be used. This requires a different tool with which to execute the action. The result is always a message indicating if the compilation is doing well or not.
Connect	The basic operation for executing and downloading the software from a repository. When the connection is made, it is possible to download the software and then compile it.

This is a brief example of a common dictionary. According to what we see in the common dictionary, we define the term and a brief description of it. This description is useful, because it tells the developer exactly what the word means and what meaning is for the business.

This knowledge is necessary in order to create good software. It allows the developer to write a good test case, which is necessary to ensure the quality required for a DSL.

Common DSL Patterns

To translate a DSL into another language, we normally, use some specific design pattern. The most common patterns are

- *Fluent interface*: The fluent interface allows the user to call a chain of connected APIs We use this technique, for example, when we call our CI process, as follows: `Connect git source control language kind "Scala"` with this call we essentially create a Fluent interface for our software.

- *Semantic model*: In DSLs, a semantic model is a representation of the structure we must parse in memory. The semantic model is essentially the connection between the object created from the grammar.

- *Parser generator*: The parser generator is used for generating the parser starting from the grammar of the DSL. The result of the parse is essentially the semantic model.

The preceding offered a brief description of some common patterns. In the next chapter, we delve deeper and try to isolate and describe the patterns that we can use for both internal and external DSLs.

Conclusion

In this chapter, I discussed the basic theory behind DSLs The two types of DSLs, internal and external, were defined, and a simple sample DSL was provided. Of course, the theory behind DSLs is very extensive, and we will go deeper into this in the following chapters. For now, some basic patterns for designing our DSL have been identified. In the next chapters, I will describe in greater detail what internal and external DSLs are and identify common patterns we can use for design.

CHAPTER 3

Internal DSL

In the previous chapter, you received a brief introduction to the different kinds of DSLs. In this chapter, you will see how to build an internal DSL. Some languages use the acronym DSL to indicate a subset of a language used in everyday life. As an example, we can think of software such as Chef or Puppet, in which it is possible to use "RubyDSL" to write the configuration files.

Creating an Internal DSL

Until now, I discussed DSLs mostly in terms of theory and presented some issues and benefits to consider when adopting DSLs. When we create an internal DSL, we have some limitations connected with the language. This means that all the expressions we create must be valid for the host language. We shouldn't forget that when we created an internal DSL, we created a subset of new instructions inside a GPL. When you think of a DSL, you must think of it as a language for creating another language.

The Ruby community uses and generates a lot of DSLs. This is because, with the metaprogramming technique, it is easy to create good DSLs. Of course, using the same techniques with another language can't yield the same results. Scala by nature has a very nifty syntax, and this allows it to create very good and clear DSLs. When we have to create an internal DSL, we normally use some specific pattern to help in the process. One of the techniques used to define an internal DSL is a *fluent interface*. We can think of a fluent interface as a synonym for internal DSL.

© Pierluigi Riti 2018
P. Riti, *Practical Scala DSLs*, https://doi.org/10.1007/978-1-4842-3036-7_3

When we consider a fluent interface, we can contemplate building a set of API functions for constructing the call in plain English. We can use some different patterns to implement this technique. The most common is *method chaining*. With this pattern, we create a "chain" of methods for calling the object.

Method Chaining

With method chaining, a set of methods is called in a chain to create an object, which is typical of object-oriented programming. Imagine, for example, that we want to create an object Student using method chaining.

```scala
case class Student(private val name: String = null , private
val year: Int = 0 ) {
  def setName(newName: String) = Student( newName, this.year )
  def setYear(newYear: Int) = Student( this.name, newYear )
  def introduce { println( s"Hello, my name is $name and I am
  on the $year ." ) }
}

object App {
  def main(args: Array[String]) {
    Student().setName("Peter").setYear(2).introduce
  }
}
```

Now we can see that we've established a chain of methods for creating an object. So, method chaining is a sequence of methods called to set the data on the object we want to create.

> **Note** In the preceding code, we used a *case class* to define our object. A case class is immutable by default and can be used in pattern matching. It's compared by structural equality, not by reference. The instantiation of a case class doesn't require the new keyword, and we can see that the definition is very succinct and simple to use.

A *case class* is very useful when we want to define immutable data. We can use the following syntax: case class User(name :String). This syntax creates a case class called User. To use the class, we can simply call and assign a value.

```scala
scala> case class User(name :String)
defined class User

scala> val user=User("Pierluigi Riti")
user: User = User(Pierluigi Riti)
```

The case class doesn't require the keyword new to be instantiated. This is because we have a method, apply, by default, and this takes care of the instantiation of the class.

The function Apply in mathematics and computer science is one that applies functions to arguments. In Scala, it is used to fill the gap between object-oriented and functional programming. For example, the function apply can override a value, as in the following:

```scala
scala> class TestApply {
    |     def apply() = "Hello World"
    | }
defined class TestApply
```

```
scala> val test= new TestApply()
test: TestApply = TestApply@3b42121d

scala> test()
res0: String = Hello World
```

Here we can see that the function `apply` is being called when we create the instance of the class, and this `Apply` is the function of the class.

With method chaining, the construction of the object is easier than with the classic construction method. Remember the term *fluent interface*? It is another name we can use for method chaining. These techniques create a cascade of methods with which to build the final object. The cascading of the object is made by each method returning an object with its parameters set. In this way, when we build the chain, we add a value to the object, and at the end, we have created a complete object.

Creating a Fluent Interface

A fluent interface for creating a chain of API calls was described by Martin Fowler and is essentially a way to change how to call an object. Traditionally, in object-oriented programming, if we want to call an object, we use a syntax such as the following:

```
Student s = new Student("Pierluigi Ri", 2);
Course c1 = new Course("Programming");
Course c2 = new Course("Mathematics");
return new Year(s, c1, c2);
```

You can see that we create the program using a set of calls, and, at the end, the final object is passed in the previously created objects. This is the classic technique every developer uses essentially every day to create objects.

If we were to use method chaining for this example, we could create a series of functions. Every function would return the object itself. In the end, we would have one complete object, the syntax of which would be the following:

```
Years()
    .student()
        .name("Pierluigi Riti")
        .class(2)
    .course("Programming")
    .course("Mathematics")
    .create()
```

The code now can be read more like plain English and is much easier to understand by a domain expert. Don't forget: The aim of a DSL is to allow the communication between a developer and domain expert. With a language such as Scala, we can use a function instead of an object, so we can use what Fowler defines as a *function sequence*. We don't use an object and a method, but only a function. With Scala, we can use this pattern and essentially build an English phrase for solving the problem.

```
Years()
    Student()
        name("Pierluigi Riti")
        class(2)
    course("Programming")
    course("Mathematics")
    create
```

The preceding string is simple to read and understand by a domain expert. This reduces the possibility of misunderstanding between the developer and domain expert and, of course, improves the quality of the software.

The essence of the fluent interface concerns how we think about and design an object. Normally, when we think of an object such as a box, we think only about how to interact with it. We may define a method and then access the method, all to create a box to solve the problem. If we think about software using a fluent interface, we approach the object differently. In this case, the object is not merely a black box. We must contemplate a new way of interacting with it. We must consider a set of commands and queries. Every command executes an action, in our example, `create`, and every query selects a set of data, in our case, the other functions. Thinking about the object in this way reflects not only a new way of defining an object but a mind switch that, in particular, enables a developer to think differently when using an internal or external DSL.

Separating the method of the object design into queries and commands is not a new way of defining software; it is a methodology of imperative programming, as elaborated by Bertrand Meyer, and takes the name *command-query separation*. The separation of command and query is based on a simple idea.

- *Query*: This returns a value but does not change the status of the system. It doesn't have side effects, thus is ideal for functional programming.

- *Command*: This changes the status of the system but doesn't return any value.

The idea behind this paradigm is to have a clear division between the function that changes the value of the system and the method reading only the state of the system. Because the system reads only an immutable state of the system, this paradigm is strictly connected with a fluent interface. With this kind of pattern, we can create a command to change the status of the system and, at the end, have a query for retrieving the status of the system following the fluent API call. Because the query is essentially without side effects, this is ideal for functional programming. The essence of the command-query separation is that *every method must return a query or a command, and the result never changes, if we don't change the initial value*. Basically, the method or function can't have side effects.

Note   The absence of side effects is one of the principles of every functional language. As Scala is a functional language, using the command-query separation doesn't violate this principle but helps the developer to respect it.

When we design internal DSLs, we must think of using this principle in order to better isolate the function or method and avoid side effects. Of course, fluent interface and command-query separation are not the same. Specifically, a fluent interface is used when dealing with objects. Conversely, a command-query separation is better for functions. Because Scala has both paradigms, it is better to define and clarify how to use one or the other. In each case, it is better to define the function or method with a name understandable to the domain expert.

Designing the Parsing Layer

Writing a good DSL requires a parsing layer. This layer is necessary to translate the formal syntax into instructions for the GPL, the general-purpose language, used to build the DSL. It doesn't matter whether we're talking about internal or external DSLs. In each case, we must create the layer.

In terms of an internal DSL, the parsing layer is strictly connected to the functions we offer for creating the DSL. When we create the parsing layer, we must think of a specific pattern. We can use *expression builders* to create the correct method for our fluent interface. An expression builder is essentially an object whose sole task is to build a model of normal objects. With expression builders, we can easily create a fluent interface.

We use expression builders because when we define our DSLs, we can have a different interface, and in such a case, it is not always easy to design a correct and fluent interface. The expression builder is our friend. Imagine that we want to create a code to save or update a new user on the system. The condition is the presence or absence of the user in the system. The code can be like this:

```scala
class InsertUser {

  private val user = new User()

  def add(name: String, surname: String): User = {
    actualUser = new User(name, surname)
    user.addUser(actualUser)
    this
  }

  def setLevel(level:String): User = {
    user.level(level)
    this
  }

  def getUser: User = user
}
```

The class InsertUser defines the object and the method. We can use the class in the following way:

```scala
val user = new InsertUser().add("Pierluigi","Riti").
setLevel("admin")
```

Now we can see that the call for creating the user can be read like plain English, and the user we created essentially is different every time we call it.

When we define an expression builder, every method returns an object, populated with the value of the method. This allows the user to create the correct fluent interface.

Another important piece of the parser is the *semantic model*. This is used to translate the grammar and the syntax defined in the DSL. This pattern creates an object in memory with all data and translates it for DSL generation. This pattern normally is used with the *symbol table*, another pattern used for defining DSLs. With the symbol table, we basically store a link between the object and each task. This is used for populating the semantic model, which is a set comprising a model and class, used for translating an input in a class. Graphically, we can imagine it to be something like that shown in Figure 3-1.

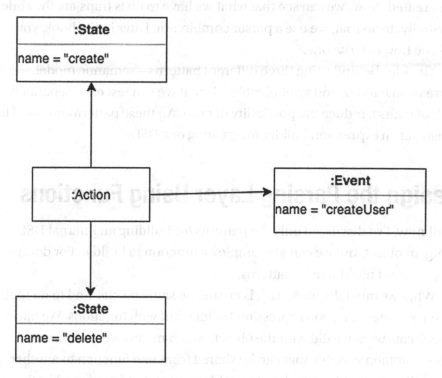

Figure 3-1. *Diagram of a semantic model*

The code to populate the model can be something like the following:

```
events
 createUser
end
state create
   createUser create
end
```

This code creates the code that can be used to represent the model we just created. Now, we can see that what we have to do is translate the code. Normally, to do that, we use a parser combinator. Later in the book, you will see how to write one.

The idea behind using three different patterns—semantic model, expression builder, and symbol table—is that we can test each separately and, of course, reduce the possibility of error. All these patterns are used to construct an expression builder for creating our DSL.

Design the Parsing Layer Using Functions

Until now, I've discussed only the patterns for building an internal DSL using an object, but we can also employ a function to build it. For doing this, we must use different patterns.

What we must do, obviously, is create the same results, and to do that, we have to create a good expression builder, but with functions. We have to replicate what we did with the object, which means we must create some common variable that can be shared from one function to another. Normally, we do this with global variables and global functions, but this is not the best way of solving the problem. Because with global functions, we can change the final result, another process can erroneously change the value of the variable, and this can change the result of our process. Imagine, for example, working in a multi-thread environment.

The best way of solving this problem is to use the pattern called *context variable*. A context variable is used to capture a value in a variable when parsing and after assigning a new one when we parse. Consider, for example, that we call a function called Course. This function must know what course Student is taking. With the context variable, we can save this value and change it when we parse the new value. Suppose, for example, that we wanted to write a class User. The class would look like the following:

```scala
class User() {
  var name = ""
  var surname = ""
  var username = ""

  def saveUser():Unit ={
        println(username)
  }
}
```

Now, we can see that the variable defined in the context can be used as the method. This is done, for example, when we want to define some specific value to send to the parser when we initialize the class. We can set the value of the variable in following way:

```scala
scala> val user=new User()
user: User = User@2001e48c

scala> user.username = "Pippo"
user.username: String = Pippo

scala> user.saveName()
Pippo
```

Of course, the variable is still global in some respects. If we want to remove the global variable completely, we can use another pattern, called *object scoping*. Every time we try to create a fluent interface, we must memorize a set of variables, to allow the fluent interface to create our final call to create the final object. We can avoid that with object scoping. With object scoping, we create a common object used to store the data. In other words, all variables are stored in a common area, and in this way, we can use them to create our final call. This means that we don't have to memorize the value in a global variable, and we can better isolate the scope of every variable. We use this technique when we create an expression builder. The method is as follows:

```
def add(name: String, surname: String): User = {
  actualUser = new User(name, surname)
  user.addUser(actualUser)
  this
}
```

This is essentially a way to isolate the variable. By doing so, there is no global variable, which reduces side effects.

The last pattern we can use for creating a fluent interface using functions is called a *nested function*. With a nested function, we build a function that can accept other functions, such as a variable. In functional programming, these kinds of functions are called higher-order functions. With a nested function, we can completely avoid the global variable and can reduce to zero any possible side effects. This way, we don't break any rules of functional programming and can improve the quality and reduce errors that can be raised by the program itself. An example of a nested function can be written as follows:

```
object NestedFactorial {
  def factorial(i: Int): Int = {
    def nestedfactorial(i: Int, accumulator: Int): Int = {
```

```
     if (i <= 1)
        accumulator
     else
        nestedfactorial(i - 1, i * accumulator)
   }
   nestedfactorial(i, 1)
 }
}
```

In this example, we define a function factorial and also that we have another function nestedfactorial. The function, in this case, executes the factorial and returned the value to the previous one. Of course, the nested function can execute completely different operations and completely change the scope. Depending on the case we execute, this technique completely isolates the core function from the outside word and essentially eliminates side effects.

Conclusion

This chapter presented a set of patterns that can be used to build internal DSLs. Every pattern offers a solution to a specific problem. Writing a good internal DSL is not simple and requires changing how we think about the API. For example, different layers must be created in order to resolve a global problem.

In this chapter, I highlighted the most frequently used patterns for designing a DSL. Future chapters will consider how to use these patterns to create an internal DSL. To create a good DSL, it is necessary to have a greater understanding of theory as well as more experience. As I have indicated, I prefer a "getting your hands dirty" approach, so I have tried to offer only a brief introduction, in order to expand later on the concepts involved in making superior DSLs.

CHAPTER 4

External DSL

External DSL is probably the most complex and, at the same time, fascinating kind of DSL. When we design an internal DSL, we establish a connection with the GPL used for defining it. With external DSLs, we define our own language. This means that we can define any kind of rules we want for the language.

Of course, when we define an external DSL, it requires more work to define the grammar and the correct rules for applying the language. This demands more effort than defining a simple internal DSL, but certainly provides more satisfaction.

Internal DSLs vs. External DSLs

First, to start to define our external DSL, I want to highlight the differences between internal and external DSLs. This will give you some idea about the design choices we must make when we talk about DSLs.

The first big difference between internal and external DSLs is connected to the limitations of the syntax of the host language. We must remember that an internal DSL is created starting from a GPL, for example, Scala. This means that we cannot use a particular word, because it is reserved for a specific language, or we cannot use some sign or syntax, because it is not valid on the host language. When we define an external DSL, on the other hand, we define our own language. This means that we rewrite all the rules for the language, valid syntax, etc.

© Pierluigi Riti 2018
P. Riti, *Practical Scala DSLs*, https://doi.org/10.1007/978-1-4842-3036-7_4

When we design an external DSL, we still de facto design a brand-new language, and we can define for it all the rules and syntax we desire. The steps we must take to implement an external DSL are the following:

- We must "read" in memory for all sources with the program.

- We must "read" in memory for the grammar.

- We must "translate" the source with the grammar.

Implementing the three preceding steps is at the core of realizing a good external DSL, but, first, we will have to define some key concepts related to external DSLs.

Grammar and Syntax

For an external DSL, the first decision we must make concerns the *grammar*. With the grammar, we start to define the set of rules that we must respect for our own language. As with any other grammar, for example, English, we define some rules to "talk" with our external DSL.

When we define the grammar, we must define the rules for the *syntax* we want our software to allow. This means, for example, defining the character for the newline, or how we can define a function or perform an operation.

The syntax is derived directly from the grammar. With the grammar, we define the rules, and the syntax is what we have after we've implemented these rules.

For defining our grammar in programming, we normally use a notation called *Backus-Naur Form*, or BNF. A BNF, in computer science, is a notation technique for defining language in a context-free grammar.

A BNF is used to define the syntax of the language. For example, we can define an address to which to send mail, in the following way:

```
<postal-address> ::= <name-part> <street-address> <zip-part>

    <name-part> ::= <personal-part> <last-name> <EOL>
                  | <personal-part> <name-part>

  <personal-part> ::= <initial> "." | <first-name>

<street-address> ::= <house-num> <street-name> <EOL>

     <zip-part> ::= <ZIP-code> <EOL>
```

If we want to write a BNF notation, we can use a definition like this:

```
<symbol> ::= _expression_
```

where <symbol> is a *nonterminal* value, and _expression_ is a sequence of one or more <symbol>s. If we have to define a choice of expression, we use the sign | in this case, meaning OR. The symbol ::= means all the values to the left should be replaced with the value to the right.

Note   By a nonterminal symbol, we indicate that every symbol can be replaced. A context-free grammar assumes that a set of the symbol can be replaced, following the rules of the normal symbol. By "normal symbol," we mean all the nonterminal terms. In this case, we wish to translate the symbol into a normal language that can be read by a human. For example, if the code is created for a postal address, the normal symbol is all symbols in quotes. The grammar defines all the rules for changing the symbols, with the final value of the language.

If, for example, we want to define a BNF for describing a CodeCommit, we can write something like this:

```
<code> ::= <language> <version> <classes> <line end>
<language> ::= "Java" | "C#"| "Ruby"
<version> ::= "0" | "1" | "2" | "3" | "4" | "5" | "6" | "7" |
"8" | "9"
<classes> ::= <character>
<character> ::= "A" | "a" | "B" | "b" | "C" | "c" | "D" | "d" |
"E" | "e" | "F" | "f" | "G" | "g" | "H" | "h" | "I" | "i" | "J"
| "j" | "K" | "k" | "L" | "l" | "M" | "m" | "N" | "n" | "O" |
"o" | "P" | "p" | "Q" | "q" | "R" | "r" | "S" | "s" | "T" | "t"
| "U" | "u" | "V" | "v" | "W" | "w" | "X" | "x" | "Y" | "y" |
"Z" | "z"
<line end> ::= "\n"
```

Using the BNF notation, we can write something like this:

```
"Java" "1" "Test"
```

Creating an External DSL

With a BNF, we can easily define our grammar, but this is not enough to create an external DSL. An external DSL requires some specific steps and components to be effective.

The BNF is used to define the grammar and write down all syntax we can use for defining our program, but we need something to translate this syntax into instructions. For doing that, we must create some layers for processing our file in an efficient way.

First, we must define a layer for a *syntactic analysis*. This translates our text and breaks down in an in-memory structure. The syntactic analysis parses the file and uses the BNF to identify every line. What is normally done is to parse the file and identify the end of the line. The first layer is responsible for creating in memory all lines required to process the execution of the program.

The first pattern we can apply to the syntactic analysis is called *delimiter-direct transaction*. Using this pattern, we split the input into chunks, usually lines, and then parse the line. The delimiter-direct transaction reads every line of the input, which can be a stream or a file in which we have defined our external DSL. Breaking this down into small chunks with the delimiter, normally, at the end of the line, or another specific character, then creates a semantic model of the DSL.

Imagine, for example, that we want to describe some action for building a continuous integration system. The code can be like this:

```
event code-commit example.cs
event code-compile start
event code-compile end
command build code
```

In this case, the parser must recognize the end of the file, to identify every single event we want to process. The parser uses the newline to identify every line. This is common to many languages and is easy for a developer to implement.

When we split the input into chunks, we have in memory every line, with enough information to define the functionality of our DSLs. For example, in the line event code-commit example.cs, we have a set of information for executing an action.

The next step for parsing our DSL is to split the line in a single command and execute it. For doing that we use a pattern called *syntax-direct translation*. What this pattern does is apply the rules of the grammar and create a syntax tree. In our case, we have created a BNF, and it is now the moment to apply the rules of the BNF for validating our input and recognize the different parts of the DSL. The syntax-direct translation doesn't define the parser but only how to apply the rules for the BNF. So, how we can translate the syntax in a parser? We can use another pattern called *recursive descent parser*. In the example of the postal address grammar, imagine that we want to parse this line: `<language>` `::=` `"Java"` `|` `"C#"` `|` `"Ruby"`. With this pattern, we create a top-down parser to translate the input syntax. So, imagine that we want to write a meta code for that. We can write something like the following:

```
boolean Language()
        if(Java())
                then true
        else if (CSharp())
                then true
        else if(Ruby())
                then true
        else
                false
```

Essentially, we create a recursive function for recognizing the nonterminal values of the syntax. Sometimes, this is enough for parsing a DSL, but if we want something more complex, we can use another pattern called *parser generator*. This pattern builds a parser driven by the grammar file defined for our DSL. This is the most complex but, at the same time, more satisfactory task when we build our DSL. Fortunately, now we have a large part of the library and software to perform this task for us, for example, ANTLR (ANother Tool for Language Recognition). With ANTLR, we can easily "design" our language graphically. The software generates the grammar for us, and what we must do after is only to parse the grammar.

Unfortunately, not all libraries are available for our language. In Scala, for example, we have an ANTLR port, but it does not have full functionality. In this case, we can use a recursive descent parser to generate our parser, without using a parser generator.

All the preceding patterns covered are used to produce the output of the DSL. We can now learn some patterns for producing the output. These patterns will help us to identify the correct strategy for the generation of our DSL.

Producing the Output

Until now, we created the parser and the parsing used for the syntax
generating the DSLs, but what we can do with the result of the parser?

The result of the parser is the basis for the next step in the process. In
reality, we introduce a solution when we mention the semantic model.
With the sematic model, we translate the input, file, or stream, and we can
use this as input for code generation.

For generating a semantic model when we parse the document, it is
possible to take two different approaches to the problem.

- *A single-step approach*: This means that we parse and
  directly generate the semantic model.

- *A two-step approach*: First, we parse the input. We then
  create a tree and, after parsing the tree, produce the
  semantic model.

If we want to use the single-step approach, we can use a pattern called
embedded translation. Using embedded translation, we create the code
directly, starting from the parser. In one call, we gradually create the
semantic model, parsing every single line of the input.

We can use this approach, because the embedded translation provides
a simple way of handling the syntax analysis and the model population.

The big problem with the embedded translation, however, is that using
the embedded translation can create a complex grammar file, because we
use only one command to translate, without using a tree to parse the file.
On the one hand, we might think that this is a good thing, but that is not
really true. The first problem involves the maintenance of the grammar. If
we have a very complex grammar, it can be difficult to maintain, especially
if we want to expand our DSL.

Another issue is related to the variable we need to memorize all the
information. Because we use a single step for parsing the grammar, we
must create some *context variable* to manage that, and this can complicate

65

the parsing. Having only one step for parsing all the grammar complicates the code that we need to generate. This is because the code needs to have in memory all the variables required for the parsing. Taking care with the parsing and being mindful of the three guidelines for creating the parser reduces the flexibility of the code. If we want to change something, we must review the entire code.

The other approach we can take is two-step parsing. In this case, we use a pattern called *tree construction*. By this approach, the parser first parses the input and produces a syntax tree. After, we parse the syntax tree and populate the semantic model.

When we create a syntax tree, we create a simple tree we can manipulate and traverse after creating the semantic model. This approach is simpler than the single step. This is because we don't use one single action to create the semantic model. Using a tree gives the developer the possibility to read the tree in a second pass and optimize the code for parsing.

Using two simple steps is better, because we can create a better test plan and, with that, a better check of the results of our parser.

In addition to that, creating two simple steps instead of one bigger one can allow for better management by the developer, and this can help to reduce time and errors.

What Is a Parser?

To translate an external DSL, we need to write a parser into the code, but what does this mean? What is a parser? By the term *parser*, we define a piece of software used to translate input into executable code.

When we create our parser, we essentially translate the input in two different stages:

- Identify the lexing
- Apply the grammar

The parser first needs to identify the lexical structure of the line we have to parse. After that, we must apply the rules of the grammar defined for the DSLs and, with the grammar, create our output.

To separate the lexing, we use the pattern *syntax-delimiter translation*. With this pattern, we essentially identify every single word from our syntax. For example, in the preceding code, we have something like this:

```
["event" , "code-commit" , "example.cs"]
```

Essentially, we create some tokens with the words of the input files, meaning that we isolate the lexer. A lexer is essentially software for performing the lexical analysis, used to create a token starting from a string. A token is essentially a part of a string or letter. When we have spilt our string, the pattern we can use to isolate the lexer is called *regex table lexer*. As the name suggests, we create a lexical analyzer, using a list of regular expressions. In this way, we can easily split the string and identify the single word of the input.

When we have identified every single word, we can begin to create the tree and apply the rules of the grammar for the language.

The next steps are checked, if the line respects the grammar of our DSL. A regular grammar is important to us, because it defines the rules for translation. If we define a good grammar, we can easily use a finite state machine to parse the grammar.

It is possible to use a finite state machine, because, essentially, with a good grammar, we can identify what is the next state of the machine, based on the actual word. Parsing is the basis of an external DSL. A good parser allows you to have a high level of maintainability of the software. Imagine, for example, we want to parse this state:

```
event code-commit example.cs
event code-compile start
event code-compile end
command build code
```

The basic function for the parser can be something like this:

```
def event : Parser[Any] = """CODE-""".r
def commit : Parser[Any] = "COMMIT"~string
def compile : Parser[Any] = "COMPILE"~string
```

This function is essentially the base for defining a parser in Scala. The state machine is essentially a set of functions called when we must translate the code.

For context-free grammar, such as that of our DSL, the best approach to translate and create the state machine is to implement a *push-down machine*. For creating this kind of state machine, we essentially create a simple state machine with an internal stack. In Chapter 6, you will see how to create a complete parser.

What Style of DSL to Use

Until now, we've seen two styles of DSLs. I highlighted how to create one style or the other, but the most important decision we must make when we implement a DSL is what kind of DSL to choose.

The difficult part in making the choice is inadequate information. More projects start without the correct level of information, and this can create problems when you need to think about what style of DSLs you must choose.

Another factor that must be considered when we make the choice is the skill of the team. If the team is not skilled at working with DSLs, what we must consider in this case is the learning curve. At first glance, an internal DSL is simpler to learn compared to an external DSL This is because for writing an internal DSL, we don't require a grammar, but only to define a set of API for solving the business problem.

On the other hand, for creating an external DSL, we have to implement all parsers for processing the input and creating the output. Of course, the power of a parser is not comparable to that of an internal DSL, but at the same time, the cost is completely different.

The best approach is to use one step or two. if we work in an Agile environment, explore the difference between the two approaches and figure out what the best one is for you. This can drive the decision and, for example, show what is the best for your work. Keep in mind that one style doesn't exclude another. You can always mix the two styles to solve the problem. The only limit is your knowledge of the different styles.

Conclusion

With this chapter, I have concluded my discussion of the theory informing DSLs. It was intentionally short, as I didn't want to overwhelm (or annoy) the reader with more theory. Starting with the next chapter, you will see how to make DSLs in practice. We will create some different projects and use these to learn how to create and use DSLs more effectively.

External DSLs are the most complex type of DSLs. To create an external DSL, we must implement our own grammar. This means that we must define every single part of the language. After that, we have to create the parser to translate our grammar into an executable software for solving our problem.

External DSLs are the most powerful of the two types of DSLs. This is because they are not restricted by the limitations of the GPL language but can have their own grammar and rules for the syntax defined by the developer.

CHAPTER 5

Web API and μService

To this point, I have presented the theory behind DSLs. In this chapter, I discuss real use cases for DSLs, starting with the realization of some web APIs and microservices.

A microservice (μservice) is the new paradigm used in web/cloud development. The reason for this lies in the nature of the microservice itself. In this chapter, I will show you how to create a microservice with Scala, using DSLs. At the same time, you will learn about microservices and how to develop and use them in Scala.

What Is a μService

The first iteration of a service architecture was service-oriented architecture (SOA). When an architect designs an SOA, he or she essentially thinks of the software as a *service,* from which every small part will be combined to build a bigger service.

When a service in an SOA is defined, normally the architect determines the level of *granularity* of the service. This means how big and how detailed the information granted by the service is. The granularity of a service in an SOA) defines how many entities it involves to return the desired information. To better explain this concept, see the following graph (Figure 5-1).

© Pierluigi Riti 2018

P. Riti, *Practical Scala DSLs*, https://doi.org/10.1007/978-1-4842-3036-7_5

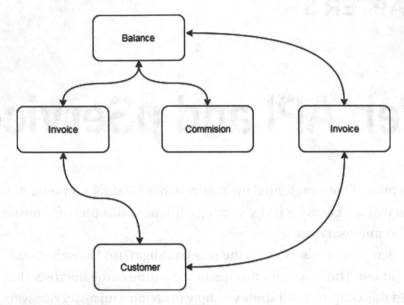

Figure 5-1. *Dissection of a service*

We can see that to maintain a balance, we must call different entities. The number of entities we call defines the kind of granularity the service has. Having a small service means having to compose more of that service to obtain the necessary information, and this is not always ideal. We create a lot of call in the back end to receive the information we need. On the other hand, having different services helps when we have to upgrade or change one of the services. If we don't change the interface, the other services basically don't care about the internal implementation of the service.

When we define a microservice, we still define a service that is *loosely coupled*. This means that the service has less interdependency, less information flow, and less coordination.

Defining a loosely coupled service system has some advantages over a system with high dependencies. First, the service has a limited knowledge of the data and low interdependency. This means that every service can be developed and used without having a big knowledge of the other service, that is, only a basic knowledge of the interface of the service we need to use. Having a loose coupling means the other service can change internally but doesn't affect our software.

A microservice is essentially just an evolution of the SOA). To design a microservice, essentially we design a service that is locally coupled. This means that we try to reduce the external dependencies on the system to improve the maintenance of the system, in case of failure. With a microservice, the system has hundreds of small services working together to solve a problem.

A microservice is a *fine-grained* service. Every service specializes in one specific aspect of the business, as the nature of the service microservice is best for designing large systems. The reason is the nature of the service itself: a microservice is intended to be small. We can think of it like a piece of Lego. Every service is a piece, and together they build a big architecture.

When we create a microservice, we must design it with three pillars in mind.

- Communication

- The team

- Innovation

When we design a microservice architecture, it can be represented graphically like in Figure 5-2.

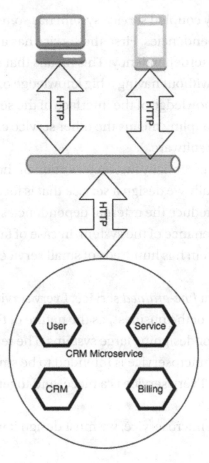

Figure 5-2. Representation of a microservice

Essentially, when we design the service, we define every single server. Every server is isolated and can be connected to a table or another service. The service is isolated, like a mini application. Now we can see how to use HTTP to establish a connection between the service and the external word.

Communication

When we design a microservice, we must make sure to have in place the correct communication practice—with the team and with other teams— because a microservice is a highly specialized service. We must be sure to have the correct communication across the team.

One of the most important principles for ensuring efficient communication is called *Conway's Law*. This study was presented for the first time in an article by Mel Conway, entitled "How Do Committees Invent?" in the *Harvard Business Review* in 1967. The most important takeaway from that study is the following:

> *Any organization that designs a system will produce a design whose structure is a copy of the organization's communica tion structure.*

Reading this simple sentence, we can understand how communication is important for design of a quality microservice. If we don't have good communication across the company, it is impossible to design a good service. It is equally true that bad communication means bad information sharing and, of course, a bad understanding of requirements.

If in practice we have bad communication, we might have some hidden dependency. This is because during meetings to discuss the service, other departments within a company can't reliably explain what they really need from the service. This can raise unexpected responses when we start to test the service, which, in turn, can translate into more time spent debugging and fixing the issue and, potentially, failure of the project.

We can take the following steps to improve communication:

- We must understand that it is normal to have separation across the teams. We don't have to fight with that, but we must spend some time working together. We must understand the natural difference and leave it at that, but at the same time, we must have a common way of communicating and resolving an issue. For example, when we design the software, we must discuss with the people responsible for maintaining the software in production what they require to solve problems efficiently.

- Use some communication tools to help improve the way we communicate with each other. For example, use tools like Slash or Skype to create virtual meetings, when is necessary. These tools reduce barriers and improve communication.

- Change the decision-making process. When we design and make a decision about the software, we must involve all company departments. This means that we must take a global decision and change what we think we know about the business. All company departments must have in mind the same idea about the business and what the final goal is.

Implementing the correct communication is one of the pillars of designing a good microservice.

The Team

The team is the second pillar for designing a good microservice. If we have a big team, for example, 20 or 30 people, it can be difficult to manage and ensure good communication in situ. On the other hand, we can really implement a system with only five or ten people.

The best solution, in the latter case, is to use Agile. Every team works with a specific microservice and, after that, uses a communication tool to share the knowledge. Having a small team work together to share information can yield faster releases and better communication across the team. In addition to that, work can be managed better, because we can understand daily how the team is doing.

Innovation

The most important reason for having good communication and a good team structure is innovation. A microservice is very good for improving a company's innovation because the nature of a microservice allows a business to have faster improvement and to reach its goals more quickly.

But how do teams and communication help? The answer is simple. Imagine that the business has a new idea, born of a new necessity resulting, in turn, from a new user requirement. If we have good communication procedures, we can easily design a new service, based on the new market requirements.

Once the proper communication is in place, and the design is complete, it is important to have an agile team that can implement the new microservice. With a small team, it is easier to distribute work and check improvements daily.

At the same time, innovation drives knowledge sharing. If a company has made innovations, usually the developer and every person involved must increase their knowledge about the service. This is positive for the company, because it improves the value of the company itself.

When to Use Microservices

The most important decision we must make regarding a microservice is when to use it. Microservices, usually the are particularly useful when we have to design large systems. This is because we can distribute work more efficiently while at the same time improving the different areas of the software. This reduces the time it takes to release the software to production.

Microservices are inherently goal-oriented. This means that when we create a microservice, we are thinking about solving a specific problem. Every service usually solves a specific problem, and these solutions can be combined to solve bigger ones.

One idea behind a microservice is its replaceability. Because a microservice is a very small service, if we have to improve or add some feature to it, it is best to replace the entire service rather than maintain or improve the existing one.

Microservices have some unique features that can help businesses to make better·decisions.

- Microservices are small in size.

- Microservices work with messages.

- Every microservice is specific for a domain context.

- Every microservice develops work independently.

- Microservices can be deployed automatically and released.

Now, we can see that microservices implement some big things. To some architects, a microservice is simply a utopia, allowing many practices to be implemented at the same time. In actuality, if we see that these practices are what DevOps solve, a company will adopt the DevOps to more easily implement the microservice.

Another big advantage of adopting a microservice is the scalability of the system. This means that the system can grow without issue. What we require, in this case, is only to build more microservices. This characteristic of microservices makes this kind of architecture ideal when we consider large companies or any company that wants to stay aligned with the market.

REST Architecture

Microservices use REST (representational state transfer) architecture to allow communication with other services. This means that REST is the basis for designing and implementing a good microservice architecture. This is because the client doesn't have to know anything about the structure of the API, only how to communicate with it.

When we create a REST architecture, we think in terms of a "resource." This means that we don't have to think only of how to use the server and how to respond to the service. We don't really care about how the API is building and what the structure is. We just think about how to call the API.

When we use a REST API, we use four HTTP methods: GET, PUT, POST, and DELETE. Every REST API uses these methods to activate the API on the server. The client makes a call for this HTTP method and sends it back as an HTTP status code. A microservice is normally built to be smaller, meaning that when we build, we design with the idea of composition and reusability in mind. Because the architecture promotes the use of a small service, a microservice is normally used with REST. This is the opposite of a SOAP (Simple Object Access Protocol) service. When we have an XML-based service, a major difference, in particular, is related to the user of the service. With a microservice, the end point is more simple to read and call. The other big difference is that building REST architecture requires fewer technology resources. Usually, when we use a SOAP, we must have a service discovery service, used to get the end point. After, we must translate the WSDL (Web Services Description Language) to an interface, and with the interface, the method for reading the data.

The REST API normally uses JSON (JavaScript Object Notation) for communicating. Of course, some services use XML, but in general, the system technology is associated with JSON. When using a REST service, we call the API, using a JSON structure, and process the response. For example, if we must *get* information about a user, we use the HTTP method GET to ask for the resource information and get back the result. If, for example, we wanted to interrogate a service using CURL, we would write the following:

```
CURL -X GET http://myservice/user/1
```

You can see that we use an HTTP method for calling the site. The response from the API will be something like this:

```
{
"id":1
"name":"Pierluigi"
"surname":"Riti"
}
```

This is a simple JSON structure and is the only response the REST API sends to the client. We can see that the JSON is a simple text file, in a structure that is readable by humans. The REST architecture is the backbone of microservices architecture.

When we talk about a REST architecture, we are referring to an architecture with some properties. The features can be summarized as follows:

- *Performance*: We design the architecture to be faster and easier to connect to. Because we use the status of the HTTP, we can immediately understand the status of the response, rather than parsing a WSDL.

- *Scalability*: Because the service is designed to be small, we can afford the horizontal or vertical scalability, which adds more to the server and deploys the service in the server.

- *Simplicity of maintenance*: Most REST web services are generally deployed in the cloud. This means that in the event of a problem, it is easy to replace the broken microservice. In the meantime, because the area of the microservice is really restricted, it is easy to isolate and fix the broken code.

- *Portability*: Because a microservice is designed to be small and usually is deployed in the cloud, data is detached from the service. This means that we can easily deploy the service in another server without losing data.

REST web services are born to be independent of one another. When we contemplate and design the service, we consider the service itself. We define one or more actions to communicate with the service, and we expose some end point. This kind of design allows the developer to use the web service without really having to know the details of its implementation. In this way, it is easy to build and reuse the web service in different contexts.

REST architecture is designed with some constraints in mind.

- *Separation of concerns*: When we define a microservice architecture, we must still define a client-server architecture. We must have a clear separation of responsibility between every single piece of the application.

- *Must be cache-free*: A microservice is normally built into a web server. This means that the information can be cached for use the next time, but when we use the microservice, we must be sure to remove the last information from the server.

81

- *Must be stateless*: When we design a microservice, we must be sure that it is stateless. This means that we don't memorize the state of the service. Every time we call, we have a new state for the service.

- *The service must be reach by a uniform interface*: The microservice is based on the Web using URIs (Uniform Resource Identifiers). To identify the service, for example, when we create a resource for an end point, we use something such as the following: `<server>/user/1`. This opens another point of our architecture.

- *The resource should be indicated in the request*: For example, when we ask for `/user`, we identify what resource we must use and what resource we want to manipulate.

- *The microservice must use the Hypermedia as the Engine of Application State (HATEOAS)*: This constriction is specific to REST architecture. It means that the client can interact with the server only via hypermedia. The client doesn't have to know anything about the server. Unlike other server applications, such as SOA) or CORBA (Common Object Request Broker), in which the client must know what protocol to use to talk with the server and what kind of information is required to send for initiating the communication, in REST, only the information matters to the client. The client sends a request via hypermedia and asks for the typical kind of result for a response. This is done by using the *content-type* specification in the request.

Using this constriction helps to design a good microservice. If we want to identify a philosophy behind the microservice, we can consider the Unix philosophy: "Write programs that do one thing and do it well."

Designing Microservices in Scala

To this point, I have presented some basic theory behind microservices, but the goal of the book is how to write DSLs using Scala. So, it is now time to dirty our hands with some code. Our guiding principal is that the microservice must allow for better transparency and communication. DSLs help the consumer of the microservice to enhance communication. How we teach the DSL is not only a technique for writing code but one for writing code that can be read like plain English. The DSLs are used to define the resource of the microservice, in particular, the principle behind the DSLs, and, internally, to write code that reads like plain English.

Scala has a fantastic framework for writing web applications. I'm referring to Play. Play is an MVC framework and can be used in Java or Scala, so the first step we must take is to install Play on our machine.

Installing the Play Framework

For installing the Play framework, we first must download it. To download the software, go to the following web address: `www.playframework.com/download`.

The best point from which to start to use Play is to download a "Starter Project." Download the zip file of the Scala project (Figure 5-3).

Play 2.5.x Starter Projects

Play Java Starter Example	Download (zip)	View on GitHub
Play Scala Starter Example	Download (zip)	View on GitHub

Figure 5-3. *Selecting a Starter Project from Play*

Unzip the file and open the folder. The structure should be something like Figure 5-4.

```
 Directory of C:\play-scala-starter-example
22/05/2017  12:17    <DIR>          .
22/05/2017  12:17    <DIR>          ..
21/05/2017  16:47               80  .gitignore
22/05/2017  12:17    <DIR>          app
21/05/2017  16:47              319  build.sbt
22/05/2017  12:17    <DIR>          conf
21/05/2017  16:47              439  LICENSE
22/05/2017  12:17    <DIR>          project
15/05/2017  10:19    <DIR>          public
21/05/2017  16:47            1,536  README.md
09/05/2017  01:44               44  sbt
15/05/2017  10:19    <DIR>          sbt-dist
09/05/2017  01:44               55  sbt.bat
22/05/2017  12:17    <DIR>          test
              6 File(s)          2,473 bytes
```

Figure 5-4. *The Play template structure*

To start a new Play project, we can execute the following simple
command, if we are in a Linux environment:

./sbt run

If we are using Windows, the command is

sbt.bat run

The command starts the sbt build, and this downloads all the
necessary files for executing the Play project.

Note   SBT (Simple Build Tool) is an open source software similar
to Maven for building projects in Scala and Java. SBT is widely used
in Scala and offers native support to build Scala code. This makes
it the preferred choice when it comes to building our Scala project.
The build descriptor is written in Scala using a specific DSL. Another
important feature is the full integration with the Scala interpreter for
faster debugging.

When sbt has finished to build the Scala project, we can see that the server is up and running.

[info] Done updating.

--- (Running the application, auto-reloading is enabled) ---

[info] p.c.s.NettyServer - Listening for HTTP on /0:0:0:0:0:0:0:0:9000

(Server started, use Ctrl+D to stop and go back to the console...)

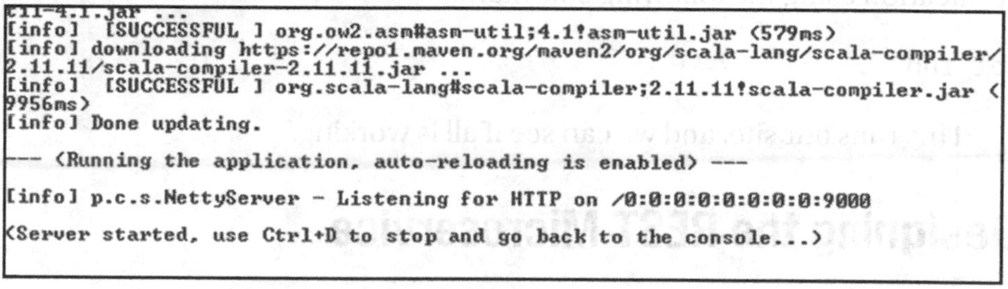

```
c11-4.1.jar ...
[info]   [SUCCESSFUL ] org.ow2.asm#asm-util;4.1!asm-util.jar (579ms)
[info] downloading https://repo1.maven.org/maven2/org/scala-lang/scala-compiler/
2.11.11/scala-compiler-2.11.11.jar ...
[info]   [SUCCESSFUL ] org.scala-lang#scala-compiler;2.11.11!scala-compiler.jar (
9956ms)
[info] Done updating.
--- (Running the application, auto-reloading is enabled) ---
[info] p.c.s.NettyServer - Listening for HTTP on /0:0:0:0:0:0:0:0:9000
(Server started, use Ctrl+D to stop and go back to the console...)
```

Figure 5-5. *The Play server up and running*

To see the Play, open the browser and call the web address http:// localhost:9000. Figure 5-6 shows the Play site.

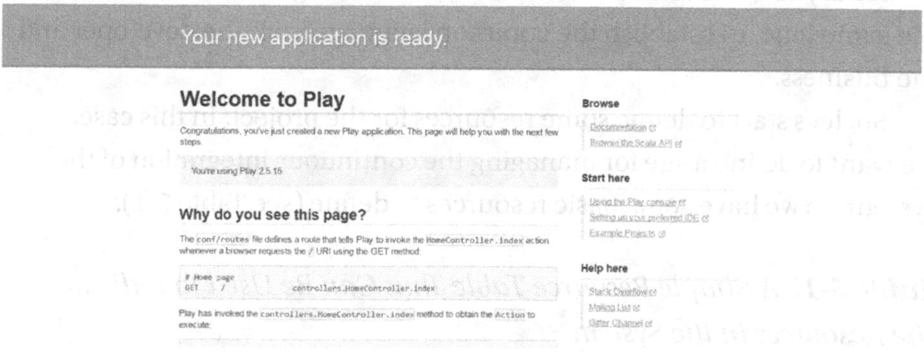

Figure 5-6. *The Play site up and running*

You can see that Play is now up and running. The next step is to create our own site for the web app and microservice. This operation is really simple and requires only a couple of commands.

First, we must create the folder from which we want to run our project.

```
media practicalscala_dsl
cd practicalscala_dsl
```

When the folder is created, we can copy into our new folder the code present in the Play folder we downloaded previously. We can run the application using the following command:

```
sbt run
```

This runs our site, and we can see if all is working.

Designing the REST Microservice

The first step is to implement the REST microservice and, of course, the web API, to design the response for every HTTP method. This helps to define the resource of the microservice and how to communicate with it.

At the same time, we create a *common dictionary*. That common dictionary can be used as well, not only for defining the resource, but, at the same time, to establish the common language from the developer and the business.

So, let's start to define some resources for the project. In this case, we want to define a site for managing the continuous integration of the system, so we have some basic resources to define (see Table 5-1).

Table 5-1. *A Simple Resource Table That Can Be Used to Indicate the Resources in the System*

Resource	HTTP Method	Response
\Language	GET	List of all languages

With Scala and Play, it's very easy to implement these resources, so the first step is to open your preferred Scala editor and create our Play project.

Creating a Microservice in Play

Creating a microservice is essentially building a web API with fine granularity. This can be done easily with Play. In the conf folder, there is a file called routes. This file is responsible for identifying the resource in the application.

```
# Routes
# This file defines all application routes (Higher priority
routes first)
# ~~~~

# An example controller showing a sample home page
GET     /
controllers.HomeController.index
# An example controller showing how to use dependency injection
GET     /count
controllers.CountController.count
# An example controller showing how to write asynchronous code
GET     /message
controllers.AsyncController.message

# Map static resources from the /public folder to the /assets
URL path
GET     /assets/*file
controllers.Assets.versioned(path="/public", file: Asset)
```

You can see that we define all resources with the HTTP method and the controller method for a response to the call.

For creating our system, we have only to add the resource on the routes files and then the method on the controller class. What we want to do is use the DSLs to create our microservice. This means that we must start from the resource. The name of the resource should be understandable by the domain experts. What we must do is write all the code in a DSL way, so let's start to write our first resource in as such. To create a microservice in Play, we essentially must build a controller to respond to the end point we have defined in the routes.

Every controller must reply to a specific end point, because the microservice is developed to be independent, but we can have a "service" use more than one controller to build the new end point. Imagine, for example, that we want to create a billing service. We can define the end point for the user, to create, update, and delete the user.

Another microservice can create a new order for the user. The microservice can create an order and use the microservice user to compose a call. All that this microservice has indicated in the route file and defined is moved to the controller part. Now, we can see that the route files have an API defined in three parts:

- The HTTP action: GET, POST, etc., is all GET in our case.
- The path of the end point: For example, /count or /message
- The controller for responding to the endpoint: For example, controllers.Assets.versioned(path="/public", file: Asset)

The controller is the central point for managing our end point, as it is the central core of the microservice. We see now how we can develop our microservice, using a real sample scenario.

Our Own DSL Microservice

The first step in creating our own microservice is to insert resources into the routes file. To do this, we add the resource name in the file. Suppose, for example, that we want to work with the language GET HTTP method. The first step is to add the route, as follows:

```
GET      /Language
controllers.LanguageController.language
```

This line defines the HTTP method GET and the action to resolve the method. So, to run the software, we must define the controller to initiate the action.

We have defined a new controller called LanguageController, which has the following code:

```
package controllers
import javax.inject.Inject
import play.api.mvc.{Action, Controller}
/**
* Created by User on 29/05/2017.
*/
class LanguageController @Inject() extends Controller{
  def language = Action{
    Ok(views.html.language("language."))
  }
}
```

This simple method responds to the GET HTTP method and returns a page. The last step, then, is to define the page that shows the result.

In Play, we can create a template to define the page. A template is defined using Scala and HTML. The controller sends the value that should be rendered in the page. For our simple page, the template looks like this:

```
@(message: String)
@main("Language Render") {
<h1>@message</h1>
}
```

We can run our application and navigate to the language to see the result (Figure 5-7).

language.

Figure 5-7. *The language page*

We will now define all our MVC (model–view–controller) routes, from start to finish. This is a simple page, so we want to use the DSL. Normally, the controller is not so simple, so we prefer to use DSLs to design the business logic and the controller only to send data that is to be rendered.

So, the business logic for this specific function is easy. We must read a configuration file and show in a table all language: active and inactive. The structure of the file is very simple. We can define it like this:

```
language.list = "Scala,Java,C"
language.status = "active,active,inactive"
```

We create a file called `language.conf`, in the `conf` folder with the language configuration. What we want now is to read the file and use it in our controller.

We can use the DSL to create a text parser to read the file and form a memory structure. We can use this structure to respond to the controller and then design the page. The code for the class follows:

```
package utils

import com.typesafe.config.ConfigFactory

final class ConfigurationReader {
        //Create the global variable for use in the parser,
        this is essentially the use for define global variable
        private var language_list = Map[String,String]()
        private var language_status = Map[String,String]()
        var result = Map[String,String]()

        //this method read the file and get the language, we
        can see how we create the map language and status
        def language() = {
                val language = ConfigFactory.load("language.
                conf").getString("language.list").split(",")
                val status = ConfigFactory.load("language.
                conf").getString("language.status").split(",")

                for(i <- 0 to (language.length - 1)){
                        this.language_list += (language(i) ->
                        status(i))
                }
                this
        }
        //this method is used for read the status of the file
        def status(status:String) = {
                if (status == "all"){
                        for((_key,_value) <- this.language_
                        list) {
```

```
                                    this.language_status += (_key
                                    -> _value)
            }
            else{
                    for((_key,_value) <- this.language_
                    list) {
                            if (_value.
                            equalsIgnoreCase(status)) this.
                            language_status +=
                            (_key -> _value)
                    }
            }
            this
    }
    //create a filter based on the status of the language,
    if there is no filter the function send out all active
    def filter():Map[String, String] = {
            this.language_status
    }
}
```

This code creates method chaining using Scala. For method chaining pattern in Scala, we need only use the word this at the end of the method.

The word this tells Scala to return the method itself, essentially, every time we return the value of the method. By doing this, we can concatenate the method and create a method chain. We use the *global variable* technique to allow the code to work with the same variable. Basically, we just define a global private variable and define the value inside the method. In this way, the object is always filled with the previous value. The object is incrementally processed, passing from method to method.

To use the method, we must change the default controller that we created to design the language view. The code for the controller is the following:

```
package controllers

import javax.inject.Inject
import play.api.mvc.{Action, Controller}
import utils._
import play.api.libs.json.Json
import play.api.libs.json._

class LanguageController @Inject() extends Controller{
        def language = Action{
                val configurationReader=new ConfigurationReader()

                val filter_language = configurationReader
                                    .language()
                                    .status("active")
                                    .filter()
                        Ok(views.html.language(filter_language.
                        toString()))
            }
}
```

The core of method chaining is this piece of code. This code is the part of the controller used to define the language controller. Now, we can define it in our end point. This controller is used to respond to the browser call: http://localhost:9000/Language. The DSL part is the "chain" we create to read the result.

```
val configurationReader=new ConfigurationReader()
val filter_language = configurationReader
                        .language()
                        .status("active")
                        .filter()
```

This code shows how to call the method in the controller, using method chaining. We can see that filtering the status of the response sets a value on the function `status`. In our case, we want only the active languages. If we now run Play, we can see the view with the filtered languages (Figure 5-8).

Map(Scala -> active, Java -> active)

Figure 5-8. *List of filtered languages*

We can see the method return a list of all languages filtered by the active status. This is exactly what we asked of our code.

We can see that it is simple to create a DSL code. In our case, we used an internal DSL pattern to compose our code. The advantage of using a DSL is related to the improvement in the communication we can have with the domain expert. Method chaining allowed the user to read the call for filtering the language like plain English.

Microservice uses JSON, so we must change how the controller works with a JSON response. We can instruct the controller to do that.

```
def language = Action{
    val configurationReader=new ConfigurationReader()
    val filter_language = configurationReader
                    .language()
                    .status("active")
                    .filter()
    Ok(Json.toJson(filter_language))
}
```

We change the response and remove the view. We use the JSON Play library to return the response in JSON. Now, if we run the code, we can see the new response on the page (Figure 5-9).

Figure 5-9. *The JSON response from the microservice*

We've now seen how to create a simple microservice and how we can view that service's reply in JSON. In our case, we have applied a filter to the microservice. If, for example, we were to ask for all languages, all languages would appear in the list. Starting from that we can format the response, but that is not within the purview of this book. The response can be read by mobile phone or any UI software.

Now, we can start to design our controller to use the DSL technique. Of course, the data source can be a database, for example. The scope of this chapter has been to show how we can use DSLs to write our controller, and how this can help us to instruct the controller output to read like plain English. This improves productivity and, of course, clarifies what the controller does.

Conclusion

We just created our first simple microservice. Essentially, we built a simple service, and we initiated a JSON response to our web service. We used simple method chaining to filter results.

This microservice is just a basic example of what we can do with Play, using only a few DSLs. Analyzing the code, we can see external DSLs. This is particularly so, because we use a configuration file to define the list of languages that we must process.

We saw how simple it is to create a DSL using the normal development process. Basically, we didn't have to consider using great complexity but only the host language, for building the most simple functionality required for the DSL. Creating a DSL should not be daunting. DSLs allow us to focus on business and communication, so simple functionality can help us to solve domain problems.

In the following chapters, we will increase the complexity of our DSL. This means that we will begin to use more complex patterns and design more complex functionality.

CHAPTER 6

User Recognition System

A common problem in building IT systems is recognizing the user and assigning to him or her the correct role. Every system has this kind of functionality, and, usually, we use a database to store the data connected to the user.

What we normally do is connect to a database, execute some query, and, with the result of the query, create a parser for understanding the role of the user.

What we want to do in this chapter is create a free grammar parser for establishing our own rules for recognizing the user. This requires that we define our set of rules and apply these to the result of the data we've gathered. This parse can be easily applied to any source, meaning that we can detach the user from a database and use a JSON or XML file for storing the user's data.

We use the Scala Parser Library to create this parser. This library is perfect for a domain specific language, so the best way to master it is to review the basics of parsers and begin to write some code.

© Pierluigi Riti 2018
P. Riti, *Practical Scala DSLs*, https://doi.org/10.1007/978-1-4842-3036-7_6

Grammar

First, to work with the Scala Parser Library, it is useful to review the basic concepts of the grammar and the theory behind a formal language. A *grammar* is a set of rules following a specific format that are used to define a string.

A grammar consists, for example, of the rules followed to write a sentence in plain English. A grammar can also be followed to write a mathematical expression, thus ensuring that the operation is executed properly and yields the desired result. Imagine, for example, that we want to define the grammar for a basic operation. We can write some rules for this, such as the following:

- Each number is an arithmetical expression.

- The basic operators we have are addition (+), subtraction (-), division (/).

- If the left and the right operators are both arithmetical expressions, we can have an operator in the middle, and this creates a new arithmetical expression.

To write the grammar, we can use the BNF (Backus-Naus Form) notation, and in this case, if we want to create a simple grammar in BNF, it would look like this:

```
digit ::=  "0" | "1" | "2" | "3" | "4" | "5" | "6" | "7" | "8"
| "9"
numbers ::= digit | digit numbers
operator ::=  "+" | "-" | "/"
expression ::= numbers | expression operator expression |
"(" expression ")"
```

Normally, to define a grammar, we use a refinement of BNF, called EBNF (Extended Backus-Naus Form). With EBNF, we can define a better compact syntax. This is the type of grammar defined in the preceding code example.

It is also possible to use the operators ? (0 or 1), * (0 or more), and + (1 or more). These operators are used in regular expressions. We can redefine the grammar using these new operators.

```
digit ::=  "0" | "1" | "2" | "3" | "4" | "5" | "6" | "7" | "8"
| "9"
numbers ::= digit | digit numbers
expression ::= term ( ("+" | "-") expression )
term ::= operation ( "\" operation )*
operation ::= number | "(" expression ")"
```

With EBNF, we can write, for example, something like (3+5)*6. This syntax is perfectly valid for our EBNF. With EBNF, we essentially define a grammar to define our "sentence." In our case, we define a new operation.

Scala Parser Combinator Library

Scala has a very powerful library for creating a parser. This library defines different kinds of parsers that we can use to write our own parser.

By "parser combinator," we mean the ability of a language to combine different parsers to create only one parser. By "parse," we mean the ability of the language to translate an input string into something different.

When we create a parser, we identify two primitives: the *element* and the *parser*. Every parser must define more than one parser element for use in "combination" for parsing the string.

Table 6-1 contains a list of the basic helper parsers we can find in Scala.

Table 6-1. *Basic Scala Helper Parsers*

Kind of Parser	Operation
Parser1 ~ Parser2	Sequencing: Using this helper tells the parser what should be checked accordingly as well as Parser2 and Parser1 of values in the input string. This means that when we use this helper, the Parser Combinator in Scala creates a sequence of objects created by the relevant part of the parser.
Parser1 | Parser2	Alternation: This checks the presence of both values Parser1 and Parser2, with a preference value of Parser1. This means that if it finds the value of Parser1, not to check the other value. Suppose we wrote something like this: 0 | 9. This would mean that the parser should check the values 0 or 9 only. All other values should not be checked by the parser. This can be assimilated to a logical operation OR.
Parser1.?	Optional: Checks for Parser1 or nothing.
Parser1.*	Repetition: Checks for each occurrence of Parser1. In case there is more than one, Parser1 returns the number of occurrences.
...	Literal: Parses a literal expression.
R	Regular expression: Uses a regular expression to create the parser. A regular expression is created, parsing every value from [and inserted between the quotation marks.
Parser1 <~ Parser2, Parser1 ~> Parser2	Sequential composition: Performs a sequential composition, starting from right to left or from left to right. This means that when we have the parser, we start from Parser1 and move to Parser2. Both values are evaluated, and the result of both parsers is what we have in response.

(continued)

Table 6-1. (*continued*)

Kind of Parser	Operation
Opt (Parser1 | Parser2)	Optional: This creates an optional parser, meaning that we can choose between two values. This is used when we make a choice about the value of the input string.
Rep (Parser1)	Repetition: This creates a parser repetition, returning a list of all occurrences detected.
Repseq (Parser1, separator)	Separated repetition: This is similar to a repetition parser, but in this case, we identify the separator for the separation. For example, we can use a comma "," to indicate the value of separation.
Parser1 ^ ^ f	Functional combinator: This creates a function with the output value of the parser.

Every parser returns a value of *success*, if the parsing operation terminates properly, or of *failure*, if the operation terminates in an error. It is possible to read this value from the object `ParserResult`. We can use this object to know exactly what's going wrong in our parser operation.

A Simple Sample Parser

Until now, I have discussed only how to create a parser combinator. What we want to do now is create a simple parser for executing some basic mathematical operation.

The parsing library defines some basic operations that we can combine to create a more complex operation. The basic operations that we can find in the library are

- Matching token
- Choosing operator (|)

- Repeat an operation (rep)

- Optionality of an operation. We can apply an operation from a choice (opt).

- Execute two operations in sequence (~).

What we do now is use the previous grammar to create a mini mathematical parser. The code is

```scala
import scala.util.parsing.combinator._

class ExprParser extends RegexParsers {
  val digit  = "[0-9]+".r

  def expression: Parser[Int] = term ~ opt(("+" | "-" )
~ expression) ^^ {
    case t ~ None => t
    case t ~ Some("+" ~ e) => t + e
    case t ~ Some("-" ~ e) => t - e
  }

  def term: Parser[Int] = factor ~ rep("/" ~> factor ) ^^ {
    case f ~ r => f / r.product
  }

  def factor: Parser[Int] = digit  ^^ { _.toInt } |
"(" ~> expression <~ ")"
}
```

We can see that the code creates a class that extends the sub-trait RegexParsers of the trait Parsers. The first step in "translating" the EBNF in the code is to define the digit. We define this by using a simple regular expression. After that, we start to define every component of our parser. In this case, we work with Int type. For this reason, every function returns a type Parser[Int].

As you can see, creating a parser with Scala is very simple. The function expression and term use both a case class to determine what kind of operation must be executed. For example, the expression checks if the values + or - are present in the expression and executes the relevant operation. Now we can see that we use the basic operator present in the library to build our operation.

To execute the parser, we must use the `parseAll` command. This method executes every parser until the end of the string. We can execute the program using the following call:

```
object Main extends App {
  val parser = new ExprParser
  val result = parser.parseAll(parser.expression, "10/2+5")
  if (result.successful) println(result.get)
  if(!result.successful) println("failure")
}
```

Note   Instead of the function `parseAll`, we can use the function `parse`, but this is not really functional. The function `parse` doesn't read all lines but stops when the first occurrence is found. For example, in our expression 10/2+5, the function `parse` exits after the command 10/2.

Defining a Domain Problem and the Grammar

As we know, a DSL exists to respond to a specific domain problem. In our case, we want to define a language that can be used to define the creation or the maintenance of existing users.

We can define some simple rules to create our language.

- The administrator can create, delete, and update users.

- An administrator can assign and/or remove roles from one or more users.

- A user can use the system according to the restrictions defined in the rules.

- The rules are "Read," "Write."

- The syntax we want to use should be similar to a JSON.

Based on these rules, we can define our EBNF, as follows:

```
value ::= objson | array | string | floatingPointNumber.
object ::= "{" | members | "}".
array ::= "[" | values | "]".
members ::= member {","  member }.
member ::= stringLitteral ":" value.
values ::= value {"," value}.
```

The grammar shows the rules for defining a new user in the system. We employ a simple JSON to define the user. This is because it is more humanly readable and simple to use for defining more complex rules. Based on the syntax, we now define a simple input for our parser.

```
{
        "Username" : [
                        {
                        "Name"   : "Pierluigi Riti",
                        "Roles" : ["Administrator", "User"],
                        "Groups" : ["Test1","Test2"],
                        "Permissions": ["All", "Read"]
                        },
```

```
                          {
                          "name" : "John Smyth",
                          "Roles" : ["User"],
                          "Groups" : ["Test1"],
                          "Permissions": ["Read"]
                          }
              ]
}
```

Using the preceding rules, we have defined two new users. You can see we've simply defined the role and used the grammar to define every aspect of the user.

Preparing the Parser

The first step we must take to create the parser is essentially to recognize the work input. To do this, we can create a simple *lexical parser*.

A lexical parser is a kind of parser specialized to recognize the lexical structure of the input. In our case, we use this parser to identify a word, split by the delimitation, and create the parser tree for creating the call in the functionality of the software. So, start to create the first version of the lexical parser, as follows:

```scala
import scala.util.parsing.combinator._

class ParserJson extends JavaTokenParsers {
  def value : Parser[Any] = obj | array |
                            stringLiteral |
                            floatingPointNumber
  def objson: Parser[Any] = "{" ~repsep(member, ",")~"}"
  def array : Parser[Any] = "[" ~repsep(value, ",")~"]"
  def member: Parser[Any] = stringLiteral~":"~value
}
```

We can execute the parser and see the response of the software. We then create the software for the call and use our JSON input file.

This is the file we use:

```
{
    "Username" : [
            {
                "Name"   : "Pierluigi Riti",
                "Roles" : ["Administrator", "User"],
                "Groups" : ["Test1","Test2"],
                "Permissions": ["All", "Read"]
            },
            {
                "Name" : "John Smyth",
                "Roles" : ["User"],
                "Groups" : ["Test1"],
                "Permissions": ["Read"]
            }
        ]
    }
```

This is the code to invoke the parser:

```
object SimpleJSONParser extends ParserJson {
  def main(args: Array[String]): Unit ={
    val reader = Source.fromFile(args[0]).getLines.mkString
    println(parseAll(value, reader))
  }
}
```

If we execute the code, we see the result of the parser.

```
parsed: (({~List((("Username"~:)~(([~List(((({~List((("Name"~:)
~"Pierluigi Riti"), (("Roles"~:)~(([~List("Administrator",
"User"))~])), (("Groups"~:)~(([~List("Test1", "Test2"))~])),
```

```
(("Permissions"~:)~(([~List("All", "Read"))~]))))~}),
(({~List(((("Name"~:)~"John Smyth"), (("Roles"~:)
~(([~List("User"))~])), (("Groups"~:)~(([~List("Test1"))~])),
(("Permissions"~:)~(([~List("Read"))~]))))~})))~]))))~})
```

Describing the Parser

What we do now is describe the parser and see what it does. At first glance, the result of the parse is not very useful for a human read. It is essentially just a sequence of lists and ~ signs. This is not exactly humanly readable but undoubtedly more readable by a computer.

A Scala parser has some rules we need to know first, to translate the output into something more useful for the computer. These are the rules:

- Each parser written as a string returns the parsed string.

- Regular expressions also return a string.

- When we have a sequential composition P~Q, this returns the result of both P and Q. These results are returned in an instance of a case class.

- When we have an alternative composition P|Q, the parse returns the result of either P or Q, depending on what element yields success.

- When the parser uses a repletion rep(P) or repsep(P, separator), this returns a result that lists all runs on P.

- When the parse runs an option opt(P), this returns an instance of the Scala's option type. It returns Some(P), in the case of success, or None, if P fails.

Using these rules, we can understand now why the result of the parser is what we have. In any case, the output is not very useful. The next step is to evolve the parser to get a structure we can use to build our own call.

Improving the JSON Parser

To make the result of the parser more humanly readable, we have to change the result of the parser a little. The most useful structure we can use is a simple Scala Map, in which the key is the name of the JSON property, and the value is the associated value.

The first step of the parser is now to create a Map when we parse the entire JSON object. The new code for the function looks like the following:

```
def objson: Parser[Map[String, Any]] =
  "{"~> repsep(member, ",") <~"}" ^^ (Map() ++ _)
```

You can see that we've changed the signature of the method. First, we use the value Any. This means that we return any value from our parser. In this case, the parser returns a value Map[String, Any]. This tells the parser to cast the result into a map of value string and any.

To make this transformation, we use a new parser operator: ^^. This operator *transforms* the result of the parser operation. To use this operator, the parser must have the syntax P ^^ r. In our case, we use a repetition control on the member, which means that we have a result transformed in a case class, and this initiates the transformation.

At the same time, we change another method to improve the parser. We change the member, as follows:

```
def member: Parser[(String, Any)] =
  stringLiteral~":"~value ^^
    { case Name~":"~value => (Name, value) }
```

For the other method, we use the operator ^^ to transform the result of the operation. In this case, we use a pattern matching to select the value Name. The entire parser code now looks like this:

```
import scala.util.parsing.combinator._

class ImprovedJsonParser extends JavaTokenParsers {
```

```scala
  def obj: Parser[Map[String, Any]] =
    "{"~> repsep(member, ",") <~"}" ^^ (Map() ++ _)

  def array: Parser[List[Any]] =
    "["~> repsep(value, ",") <~"]"

  def member: Parser[(String, Any)] =
    stringLiteral~":"~value ^^
      { case name~":"~value => (name, value) }

  def value: Parser[Any] = (
    obj
      | array
      | stringLiteral
      | floatingPointNumber ^^ (_.toDouble)
  )
}

object ImprovedJsonParserTest extends ImprovedJsonParser {
  def main(args: Array[String]) {
    val reader = "{\n\t\"Username\" : " +
      "[{\"Name\" : \"Pierluigi Riti\"," +
      "\"Roles\" : [\"Administrator\", \"User\"]," +
      "\"Groups\" : [\"Test1\",\"Test2\"]," +
      "\"Permissions\": [\"All\", \"Read\"]" +
      "}," +
      "{\"Name\" : \"John Smyth\"," +
      "\"Roles\" : [\"User\"]," +
      "\"Groups\" : [\"Test1\"]," +
      "\"Permissions\": [\"Read\"]}]} "
    println(parseAll(value, reader))
  }
}
```

If we execute the code, we actually have a result like the following:

```
Map(
        "Username" -> List(
              Map(
                        "Name" -> "Pierluigi Riti", "Roles" ->
                        List("Administrator", "User"),
                        "Groups" -> List("Test1", "Test2"),
                        "Permissions" -> List("All", "Read")
              ),
               Map(
                        "Name" -> "John Smyth",
                        "Roles" -> List("User"),
                        "Groups" -> List("Test1"),
                        "Permissions" -> List("Read")
               )
        )
)
```

We can see the result is now more readable to humans than the previous result. We finally realize that our own parser is using an external DSL to define it. When we create an external DSL, we have a set of patterns that we can use to generate a parser. We have, for example, a *parser generator* pattern, and this is exactly what we use here. This pattern uses an external grammar to generate the language. An external DSL essentially generates a code used as an external source. In this case, we use a JSON file. A JSON file offers us the grammar we need to read and parse to generate the code.

We can use different techniques for parsing the file. In this case, I used a short introduction and a JSON, but we can create more complex parsers using DSLs. For example, we can create a *syntax-directed translation*. This pattern translates a source, normally a text, by defining a grammar and then using this grammar to create a structured translation. We see the use of this pattern, for example, when we translate the EBNF into a software. We take a grammar, the EBNF, and then generate an input, based on the grammar. The software gets the grammar and then translates the source into software.

This parse uses a JSON format notation, which allows us to create our grammar. This is because it is easy to parse and create our own syntax for the software we want define.

What we have learned until now is sufficient to start to create our own simple parser, but we need to know what element we used to create the parser (see Table 6-2).

Table 6-2. *Parser Operator Used to Create Our Simple JSON Parser*

Operator	Description
…	Literal
"…".r	Regular expression
P~Q	Sequence of composition
P<~Q , P~>Q	Sequence of composition: follow only move left/right
P | Q	Alternative: the result is P or Q
opt(P)	Optional: in case of success P
rep(P)	Repeat the parser on P
repsep(P,Q)	Interleaved repetition
P ^^ f	Result of the conversion

In the preceding table, we see how many combinator parsers use symbolic names to describe an operation, for example, <~ or ^^.

This notation has the big advantage of being compact to write but, on the other hand, is difficult to remember and can be very cryptic for people with little experience. The big advantage of using a symbolic name is the short length of the code and the possibility of implementing the correct precedence in the parser itself.

What we have created until now is an in-memory parser. We can use this parser to develop a sequence call of methods to execute operations on the system. For example, we can create the function and use it to update a table in a database or file system.

Conclusion

In this chapter, you received a brief introduction to the Scala's Parser Combinator Library. This library is very powerful and can be used to create equally powerful code.

We scratched only the surface of the Parser Combinator Library, but in spite of that, we were able to create a powerful parser to read and create in memory three others with the structure of the code.

In the next chapter, you will see how to a create more complex parser, when I cover the rest of Scala's Parsing Combinator Library.

CHAPTER 7

Creating a Custom Language

So far, we have gone little by little deep inside the DSL. At this stage, we are able to create external and internal DSLs. In this chapter, we go deeper into external DSLs and begin to develop a custom language.

A lot of software has an internal language. An example is RubyDSL used in Chef to produce cookbooks. This language started from a GPL language and, with a DSL implementation, became a new language. The language is normally used to solve a specific issue. In the case of Chef or Puppet, we use a "new language" to automatically install patches and software in the system.

The language we create can be of any scope we have in mind. We can create, for example, a language exclusively for math or to "copy" another language. In our case, we want to create a language similar to the old BASIC.

In this chapter, I will discuss the general rules for creating our own language. Of course, we don't have a compiler, so it will not be an actual new GPL language. What we want is to create a new language based on Scala. For doing this, we must learn to write an AST, *Abstract Syntax Tree*, to parse in memory the command and then execute the function. But, first, to start with the implementation, it is best to cover a little bit of theory.

© Pierluigi Riti 2018
P. Riti, *Practical Scala DSLs*, https://doi.org/10.1007/978-1-4842-3036-7_7

What Is a "Language"?

By *language* we mean a *syntax* that respects a *grammar* used to define a set of words that we can combine to communicate and solve a problem.

When we define a language, we define a set of rules we can use to define our own language structure. This can be used to solve some specific problems.

We use language every day of our lives when we talk in English or Italian or French. We use a set of words connected to respect a specific grammar to build a phrase understandable by every person who knows our same syntax and grammar.

What we write is a programming language. By the term *programming language*, we define a *formal language* used to define a set of instructions to produce an output. Every programming language is normally defined by two components.

- *Syntax*: How to write the language, what words are basic to the language, such as if… then, for loop, etc.

- *Semantics*: What the language means, for example, when we write for or if then

Every programming language is used to solve an algorithm. When we use the language, we use the syntax to define a semantic specific to solving a particular algorithm.

The first step we must take to define our own language is to define the syntax we want our language to use. By syntax, we mean all the words and the rules we combine to design the semantics of the language.

For example, we must define reserved words, the words we use specifically for the language, for example, to identify the end of the line or if we have an if…else.

Patterns for Designing a Language

When we design a language, we must consider many of its aspects. We must define the grammar, the syntax, and think about how we can translate the input into instructions.

There are some specific phases we must initiate to correctly translate an input into a language.

1. Recognize the syntax and build the IR, intermediate representation. This is done by a reader.

2. Execute the semantic analysis. This is done through an interpreter.

3. Generate the language. This uses a translator.

4. Produce the output.

All these phases are important when we want to build our own language. As you can see, we have essentially three macro components in every phase. This component is basic to every language parser. Now, we can try to describe the components.

- *Reader*: The reader is responsible for building a data structure from the input. Essentially, the reader is where the input is translated into a data structure.

- *Interpreter*: The interpreter walks through the structure created by the reader and executes the operation.

- *Translator*: The translator is a combination of the reader and interpreter. Basically, it receives an input and produces an output.

To implement all the phases, we can use different patterns. The principal pattern we can use are *recursive descent recognizers*. These are used to translate phrases and sentences into the basic grammar of the language.

The most basic and used reader component is the *recursive descent lexer*. This pattern creates a set of tokens from a character that is used to recognize the words of the language. This pattern is normally used with the recursive descent recognizers to create the parser. Suppose we want to parse an expression. We can design the parser in the following way (Figure 7-1).

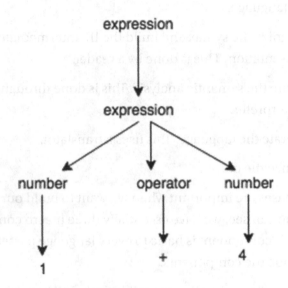

Figure 7-1. *A tree syntax grammar*

Now, we can see that we start from the basic expression 1+4. This is the first input. Next, the expression goes through another step and is split into individual parts. At this point, every single character is split into parts, such as operators and numbers.

This pattern is basic to most language parsers, but the starting point of every parser is to define the three components of the syntax. The common pattern for doing that is called an *abstract syntax tree (AST)*. With an AST, we create a node for every important token used in the grammar. The AST is built using the classic three-node structure. To create the AST, we can use two different patterns.

- We can use the parse tree pattern. This pattern describes how to recognize the input sentence and parse it. The following diagram (Figure 7-2) illustrates this. Now you can see how we check the operator. As the numbers descend, the parser terminates the start of the operation and applies the operation to the number.

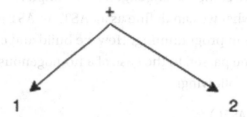

Figure 7-2. *The parser applied to a specific function, in this case the function + with the two parameters*

- Another pattern we can use is the homogenous AST. This kind of pattern has a simpler implementation than the previous one. In this pattern, we implement an AST using a single-node data type, and we normalize it after the child list represents a diagram similar to the following (Figure 7-3).

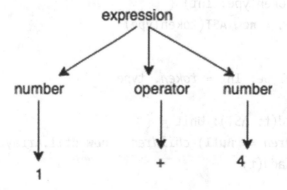

Figure 7-3. *Homogenous AST tree parser*

117

This pattern spits the first node directly into a subset of children. Every child is a representation of a part of the expression that we must parse.

We can normalize the node using a *normalized heterogeneous AST*. This is used for trees having a multitude of node types and/or when we want to develop a homogenous AST with more than a single-node data type. But all children can be normalized. A homogenous AST is used when we have more complex languages, for example. All the parsers have in common what we can define as an AST. An AST is essentially a tree—nothing new in programming. How we build and create the tree is how we define the parser. In the case of a homogenous AST, we have something like the following:

```scala
class HomogenousAST()
{
  var token:ParserToken = null

  var children:List[ParserToken] = null

  def this(token: ParserToken) {
    this()
    this.token = token
  }
  def apply(tokenType: Int) {
    this.token = new AST(tokenType)
  }

  def getNodeType: Int = token.`type`

  def addChild(t: AST): Unit = {
    if (children == null) children = new util.ArrayList[AST]
    children.add(t)
  }
}
```

Another pattern we can use to create an AST is the *irregular heterogeneous AST*. This pattern is the most complex of the three, as it uses more than one node. These nodes are not all regular and have different child representation. This pattern differs from the homogenous AST in that names have a name. Usually, the pattern is a linked list. We can define the pattern this way:

```
var previous:ParserNode
var next:ParserNode
    def addingNode(previous:ParserNode, next:ParserNode):Unit =
{
        this.next = next
        this.previous = previous
    }
```

All these patterns can be used to create our AST. They are the basis for creating a tree that we can walk to create our language. To walk a tree, we can use another specific pattern for doing so. Every pattern has a different use. Following is a brief list of these:

- *Embedded heterogeneous tree walker*: This pattern walks through a hetcrogeneous AST using a recursive function. A pseudo code for this parser follows. Here we can see that the actual node is derived from the root, then we identify the operation of the actual node and execute the operation. After that, we begin to read the other children of the actual node.

```
class <ActualNode> extends <root>
{
        def <node operation>():Unit = {
                <basic operation for this level of tree>
                <read the children>
        }
}
```

- *External tree visitor*: This pattern creates a visitor class, used to walk through the tree nodes. This pattern follows the same logic as the embedded version. The only difference is that the code is external, so we call another class to do the walking. We can define a pseudo code like this:

```
trait <Node>
{
        def operationNode()
        def numberNode
}
```

- Now what we see is essentially an interface in which every part defines a way to read the node.

- *Tree grammar*: This pattern is used to create the external visitor. This pattern essentially defines the grammar we must use for the external visitor. This is normally done with ANTLR. An example of the grammar to define an operation could be as follows:

```
match(operation);
match(number);
match(operation);
```

- This grammar is used to identify the piece of the tree grammar used for the parser.

- *Tree pattern matcher*: This pattern is used to trigger an action when it finds some term relevant to the pattern. This pattern doesn't have a real implementation but is a way of translating graphically how the parser is working. We can see an example of this pattern when we design the grammar for the different parser, as shown in Figure 7-4.

120

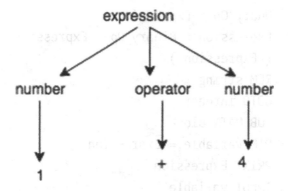

Figure 7-4. *A tree pattern matcher generator*

All these patterns are used when we want to build our external DSL. In the end, when we create our own language, we must still create an external DSL. We take an input and parse it to create a specific output.

Designing the Language

So far, we have defined the different patterns we can use for parsing the language, but there is another step we must define when we design a new language. The first decision must make is the syntax for the language. To define the syntax and the grammar, we use the EBNF language. The language we want to design is similar to the BASIC language, so the EBNF is like this:

```
Unary_Op       ::=     -    |    !
Binary_Op      ::=     +    |    -    |    *    |    /    |    %
      |        =    |    <    |    >    |    <=    |    >=
|    <>
      |        &    |    '    |    '
Expression     ::=     integer
      |        variable
      |        "string"
```

121

```
            |        Unary_Op    Expression
            |        Expression    Binary_Op    Expression
            |        ( Expression )
Command ::=          REM string
            |        GOTO integer
            |        SUB MAIN block
            |        DIM variable = Expression
            |        PRINT Expression
            |        INPUT variable
            |        IF Expression THEN integer

Line    ::=          integer Command

Program ::=          Line
            |        Line Program

Phrase  ::=          Line | RUN | LIST | END
```

Here, we define every single element of our language. Remember:
We want to try to re-create a BASIC language, so we use the syntax of the
elder BASIC. Essentially, we define every single part of the language. This
definition gives to us the model to create the basis of the language.

Using the grammar described previously, we can write a program such
as this:

```
PRINT "Table of Squares"
PRINT
PRINT "How many values would you like?"
INPUT num
```

Creating the Language

With the grammar defined, we can start to create our language. First, starting with our language, we can identify three major components for our parser.

- *The reader*: Essentially, the parser in which we define all grammar and reserved words. This creates an AST.

- *The interpreter*: This walks the AST created in the reader.

- *The translator*: Some Scala classes use this to translate the result of the interpreter in an output.

When we define the parser, we must use the reserved words of the language, so let's start to create the Reader class.

Creating the Reader Class

The core of our parser is the Reader class. This class extends the StandardTokenParsers of Scala. This is the backbone for our parser. We start by creating the reserved words used by the language, as follows:

```
class Reader extends StandardTokenParsers {
  lexical.reserved += ("DIM", "PRINT", "IF", "SUB", "THEN",
"FUNCTION", "SUB", "MAIN", "RETURN", "END FUNCTION")
  lexical.delimiters += ("*", "/", "%", "+", "-", "(", ")",
"=", "<", ">", "==", "!=", "<=", ">=", ",", ":")
```

You can see that we first define all the reserved words and delimiters that will be used by the Scala parser. These are the words we can use to tokenize our language.

As noted earlier, we can use different techniques to create our AST, so we have to define the rules we must apply to our language. These rules are used to create the tree we can use later to translate the language. To compile the rules, what we need to do is translate the EBFN that we have defined in Scala syntax.

The first rule we want to establish is the entry point for our program. In BASIC, this is usually the SUB MAIN. The code for this is as follows:

```
def mainPoint: Parser[Program] = (rep(function) <~ ("SUB" ~
"MAIN")) ~ block ^^ {
  case f ~ c => new Program(f, c)
}
```

We can stop for a moment to analyze this first function. We can see that this function uses the element that I introduced in Chapter 6.

```
(rep(function) <~ ("SUB" ~ "MAIN")) ~ block
```

The program has a number of functions that can be repeated. After the word SUB MAIN, we find a *block*. This is essentially another part of the rules, and it identifies the block of code we can write inside the main function. We can now continue to write other simple rules for defining the language.

```
/*
with this function we define the node "function" this node is
created when we found the word FUNCTION(), we build essentially
a complex node, we have FUNCTION, and some argument, after
the () we expect a "block" and optiona a return statement,
this function use the Helper parser define in the chapter 6,
the function want and END FUNCTION for close it. The block is
something like that:
FUNCTION Test()
  PRINT "Test"
END FUNCTION
```

```
*/
def function: Parser[Function] = ("FUNCTION" ~> ident) ~ ("("
~> arguments) ~ (")" ~> block) ~ opt(returnStatement) <~ "END
FUNCTION" ^^ {
  case a ~ b ~ c ~ None => new Function(a, b, c, Number(0))
  case a ~ b ~ c ~ d => new Function(a, b, c, d.get)
}

//With this function we define the RETURN word, used in the
FUNCTION method
def returnStatement: Parser[Expr] = "RETURN" ~> expr ^^ {
  e => e
}

def arguments: Parser[Map[String, Int]] = repsep(ident, ",") ^^
{
  argumentList => {
  (for (a <- argumentList) yield (a -> 0)) toMap
  }
}
//This function defines a block, the block is a set of
statements used to define the functionality of the code
def block: Parser[List[Statement]] = rep(statement) ^^ { a => a
}

def statement: Parser[Statement] =
positioned(variableAssignment | outStatement | ifStatement |
executeFunction | outStatement) ^^ { a => a }
//This defines the reserved word DIM used to define the
variable
def variableAssignment: Parser[VariableDefinition] = "DIM" ~>
ident ~ "=" ~ positioned(executeFunction | expr) ^^ { case a ~
"=" ~ b => { new VariableDefinition(a, b) } }
```

125

```
def outStatement: Parser[PrintStatement] = "PRINT" ~>
positioned(expr) ^^ { case a => new PrintStatement(a) }
```
//This defines the statement if, this means when the code finds
an if, now we can see we found the code conditional ~ block
this means we must use the function conditional to define the
word to use, this is essentially a node, with a definition of
child inside
```
def ifStatement: Parser[IfStatement] = conditional ~ block ^^ {
  case a ~ b ~ c => {
    c match {
      case None => new IfStatement(a, b, List())
      case _ => new IfStatement(a, b, c.get)
    }
  }
}
```
//This defines a conditional statement used in the block of
code, now we can see in the word IF( ) THEN we can define some
condition, the code can be IF(TRUE)THEN
```
def conditional: Parser[Condition] = "IF" ~ "(" ~> condition <~
")" ~ "THEN"
```
//the condition, is used to define the operator we can use in
the if , for example ==, > or < the if now can be write //like
that:
// IF (VALUE==TRUE)THEN
```
def condition: Parser[Condition] = positioned(expr) ~ ("<" |
">" | "==" | "!=" | "<=" | ">=") ~ positioned(expr) ^^ {
  case a ~ b ~ c => {
    new Condition(b, a, c)
  }
}
```

```
def iterations: Parser[Int] = numericLit ^^ { _ toInt }
//This essentially is responsible for parsing the FUNCTION,
what we do is use the Parser Helper from Scala and call
the function involved, this helps to translate the code in
functionality
def executeFunction: Parser[CallFunctionMethod] = ((ident) <~
"(") ~ callFunctionMethod <~ ")" ^^ {
  case a ~ l => new CallFunctionMethod(a, l)
}

def functionCallArguments: Parser[Map[String, Expr]] =
repsep(functionArgument, ",") ^^ {
  _ toMap
}

def functionArgument: Parser[(String, Expr)] = (ident <~ "=") ~
expr ^^ {
  case a ~ b => (a, b)
}
//This function executes a parser of the operation, apply the
operation + or - to a term, the term is a number used to create
the operation, we can see in this case another little piece of
parser kept alive
def expr: Parser[Expr] = term ~ rep(("+" | "-") ~ term) ^^ {
  case a ~ List() => a
  case a ~ b => {
    def appendExpression(c: Operator, p: Operator): Operator =
{
      p.left = c
      p
    }
```

```
    var root: Operator = new Operator(b.head._1, a, b.head._2)

    for (f <- b.tail) {
      var parent =
        f._1 match {
          case "+" => new Operator("+", null, f._2)
          case "-" => Operator("-", null, f._2)
        }

      root = appendExpression(root, parent)
    }

    root
  }
}
//This function defines a term, essentially identify every
single part of an expression
def term: Parser[Expr] = multiplydividemodulo ^^ { l => l } |
factor ^^ {
  a => a
}

def multiplydividemodulo: Parser[Expr] = factor ~ rep(("*" |
"/" | "%") ~ factor) ^^ {

  case a ~ List() => a
  case a ~ b => {
    def appendExpression(e: Operator, t: Operator): Operator =
{
      t.left = e.right
      e.right = t
      t
    }
```

```
  var root: Operator = new Operator(b.head._1, a, b.head._2)
  var current = root

  for (f <- b.tail) {
    var rightOperator =
      f._1 match {
        case "*" => Operator("*", null, f._2)
        case "/" => Operator("/", null, f._2)
        case "%" => Operator("%", null, f._2)
      }

    current = appendExpression(current, rightOperator)
  }

    root
  }
}
def factor: Parser[Expr] = numericLit ^^ { a => Number(a.toInt)
} |
  "(" ~> expr <~ ")" ^^ { e => e } |
  ident ^^ { new Identifier(_) }
```

The preceding code represents all the code for the Reader. We write the code to parse every element of the language, and we introduce the concept we used to create the parser. Essentially, we split every single command, for example, the if or the function, in a piece of code used to create a token. We essentially tokenize the element. With this element, we can create the AST. We can now define the last function for the language and close the reader. We must implement the function parseAll from the trait we have extended for starting the parser, as follows:

```
def parseAll[T](p: Parser[T], in: String): ParseResult[T] = {
  phrase(p)(new lexical.Scanner(in))
}
```

The function parseAll calls the lexical.Scanner and creates the parser for our language. This function creates the token for every element of the language.

This piece of code introduces some elements we must develop for creating the language. Basically, we create a call from some structure we need to define to generate the output of the reader. This code solves the first step of our parser and addresses the first requirement of the creation of our own language. The next step is to create the translator. This is not a simple class but a branch of the class used to translate the language. First, to describe the translator, we must define how the code builds the AST.

Defining the Token

For building the AST in memory, we must define the token used to create the AST. This is the first step to translate our code into something else.

These classes are used to define every single operation we have in our language. To build our AST, we start to create the basic class Expr and the trait Statement, as follows:

```
import scala.util.parsing.input.Positional

trait Statement extends Positional
```

The preceding code shows the trait Statement. This class is used by the other class to generate the token. We thus create a set of classes we can use to parse every single operation in the language. A trait in Scala is similar to an interface in Java or other languages. In this case, the trait defines an interface we can use to define the parser. In this case, we extend a Positional method. This specific trait is used when we want to define a specific position for an element of the language. Imagine, for example, that we want to define an If. We must have in an exact position the element we want to check. In this case, the trait Positional helps us to define exactly that.

We generate a class for every command, for example, the If statement is defined in this class, as follows:

```
package practical.dsl.parsers.model
```

```
case class IfStatement(condition: Condition, trueBranch:
List[Statement], falseBranch: List[Statement]) extends
Statement
```

We can see that the class extends the Statement trait and uses a case class to define the functionality. Using this kind of technique to create the parser allows us to create an AST in a simple way. The only class that doesn't use the Statement trait is the Expr class.

```
package practical.dsl.parsers.model
```

```
import scala.util.parsing.input.Positional
```

```
class Expr extends Positional
```

```
case class Number(value: Int) extends Expr
```

```
case class Operator(op: String, var left: Expr, var right:
Expr) extends Expr
```

```
case class Identifier(name: String) extends Expr
```

This class is used to define every operation in the language. We define the Number, the Operator, and the Identifier. The Expr class extends the Positional trait. This trait gives the position of the object. Essentially, we can identify the object of every single object in the code. This is useful if we want to translate the software in an operation.

Creating the Translator for the Language

The Translator class is the starting point for translating our AST into something different. The code for the Translator follows:

```
class Translator(program: Program) {
  var currentScope = new Scope("global", null)

  def run() {
    walk(program.statements)
  }

  private def getVariable(ident: Identifier): Expr = {
    var s: Scope = currentScope

    while ((!s.name.equals("global")) && !s.variables.
    contains(ident.name)) s = s.parentScope

    if (s.variables.contains(ident.name)) s.variables(ident.name)
    else {
      sys.error("Error: Undefined variable " + ident.name )
    }
  }
//With this method we want to identify what operation we can
apply to the number
  private def calculateExpr(e: Expr): Int = {
    e match {
      case Number(value) => value
      case Identifier(name) => {
        calculateExpr(getVariable(e.asInstanceOf[Identifier]))
      }
      case Operator(op, left, right) => {
        op match {
```

```scala
        case "*" => calculateExpr(left) *
calculateExpr(right)
        case "/" => calculateExpr(left) /
calculateExpr(right)
        case "%" => calculateExpr(left) %
calculateExpr(right)
        case "+" => calculateExpr(left) +
calculateExpr(right)
        case "-" => calculateExpr(left) -
calculateExpr(right)
      }
    }
  }
}

  private def isConditionTrue(condition: Condition): Boolean =
{
    val a = calculateExpr(condition.left)
    val b = calculateExpr(condition.right)

    condition.op match {
      case "==" => (a == b)
      case "!=" => (a != b)
      case "<=" => (a <= b)
      case "<" => (a < b)
      case ">=" => (a >= b)
      case ">" => (a > b)
    }
  }

  private def executeFunction(f: Function, arguments:
Map[String, Expr]) {
    currentScope = new Scope(f.name, currentScope)
```

```
    for (v <- arguments) currentScope.variables(v._1) = v._2

    walk(f.statements)

    currentScope = currentScope.parentScope
}
  private def walk(tree: List[Statement]) {
    if (!tree.isEmpty) {
      tree.head match {
        case FunctionCall(name, values) => {
          val f = program.functions.filter(x => x.name == name)

          if (f.size < 1) sys.error("Error: Undefined function
          '" + name + "'")
          else {
            executeFunction(f(0), values)

            walk(tree.tail)
          }
        }
        case Variable (name, value) => {
          if (value.isInstanceOf[FunctionCall]) {
            val functionCall = value.asInstanceOf[FunctionCall]
            val function = program.functions.filter(x => x.name
            == functionCall.name)

            if (function.size < 1) sys.error("Error: Undefined
            function '" +
              functionCall.name + "' being called at position
              [" +
              tree.head.pos.column + "] on line: " +
              tree.head.pos.line)
            else {
```

```
          executeFunction(function(0), functionCall.values)

          currentScope = currentScope.parentScope

          currentScope.variables(name) = function(0).
          returnValue
        }
      } else {
        currentScope.variables(name) = value
      }

      walk(tree.tail)
    }
    case PrintStatement(value) => {
      println(calculateExpr(value))
      walk(tree.tail)
    }
    case IfStatement(condition, trueBranch, falseBranch) => {

      if (isConditionTrue(condition)) walk(trueBranch) else
      walk(falseBranch)

      currentScope = currentScope.parentScope

      walk(tree.tail)
    }
    case _ => ()
  }
 }
 }
}
```

The translator uses the token created by the AST to walk through the tree. For the translator, we essentially use a walk tree pattern. The different tokens are created with the AST and are defined in the model. The model is essentially the plain class used to create the syntax.

The interpreter basically implements an external tree visitor pattern. We use the class to create in the model a package to read AST and translate it into a language. The class involved is a plain Scala class, and taken together, they are designed for translating the input as an output.

At the core of all the translators is the walk function. This implements the pattern. The function gets the tree, a list of statements, and checks every statement and calls the class for translating the AST into a language.

Executing the Language

The last step we must take is to create the code to execute the language. An object is responsible for reading the input file and calling the parser. The relevant code follows:

```scala
object Language {
  def main(args: Array[String]) {
    val inputFile = Source.fromFile("source/practical.bascala")
    val inputSource = inputFile.mkString

    val parser = new SmallLanguageParser
    parser.parseAll(parser.program, inputSource) match {
      case parser.Success(r, n) => {
        val interpreter = new Interpreter(r)

        try {
          interpreter.run
        } catch {
          case e: RuntimeException => println(e.getMessage)
        }
      }
      case parser.Error(msg, n) => println("Error: " + msg)
      case parser.Failure(msg, n) => println("Error: " + msg)
      case _ =>
```

```
    }
  }
}
```

The code is very simple. It calls the input file, `practical.bascala`, and executes it to get the result. The file input is the following:

```
FUNCTION printVoid()
    PRINT "Hello World"
END FUNCTION

SUB MAIN
    printVoid()
END SUB
```

Conclusion

In this chapter, we delved further into external DSLs. We created a new language using an external DSL, and you saw that this can be fun if not always easy.

You learned about the different kinds of patterns for implementing the language and the three main objects involved. Finally, we created our own parser and language.

Of course, this is only a simple example of a language, but we discovered more interesting techniques related to external DSLs and using the Parser Combinator of the Scala language. You can now easily create your own language, and this can be used for our project.

CHAPTER 8

Mobile Development

Mobile development has taken on more importance in everyday development. An ever-increasing number of companies now has mobile development teams. In this chapter, you will learn the basics of mobile development and how to use Scala and DSLs to create your own applications.

Introduction to Mobile Development in Android

Android is an open source operating system developed by Android, Inc., later a subsidiary of Google. The nature of Android allows a developer to use the same source code for different devices, for example, a desktop computer or mobile phone.

Android is not just an operating system but an ecosystem. The community offers you tools for total development. Android is a game-changer in the mobile community. To understand why Android is becoming so important to the technology community, it is necessary to understand the history of mobile software development.

The first mobile development was essentially based on a proprietary operating system. For development, all the mobile companies defined and released WAP, the Wireless Application Protocol, a technical standard

© Pierluigi Riti 2018
P. Riti, *Practical Scala DSLs*, https://doi.org/10.1007/978-1-4842-3036-7_8

used to define web navigation. With WAP, it was possible to initiate web development for mobile. Every company released a WAP browser, which allowed developers to create the first mobile site. Nokia was the first to improve the development. With Nokia, we begin to have our own framework, and this allowed developers to create their own games. Following Nokia, other companies developed their own libraries for mobile development. Of course, the software was proprietary and could only be used in phones made by the corresponding brand.

When Android was born, it allowed developers to create better applications for a large number of devices, without much change to the code. For Android development, Google released Android Studio, a tool to develop Android applications in a simple way. We will use this tool to develop our Scala application, so first, we must install Android Studio.

Starting with Android Development

To begin Android development, the first step is to download the SDK (Software Development Kit). The new version of Android SDK is connected to Android Studio. This is an editor based on JetBrains IntelliJ. The link for downloading the SDK is `https://developer.android.com/studio/index.html`.

Download the software for the correct operating system and follow the instructions for installing Android Studio. When Android Studio is installed and started, you will see something similar to Figure 8-1.

Figure 8-1. *The Android Studio start page*

To begin our Scala Android project, we must install Scala Plugin), by selecting Plugins from the Configure menu (Figure 8-2).

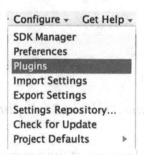

Figure 8-2. *The Configure menu*

From the Plugins menu, select Browse From Repository, and then, in the new menu, write Scala. This will show all plug-ins in Scala. Select the plug-in) Android Scala, as shown in Figure 8-3.

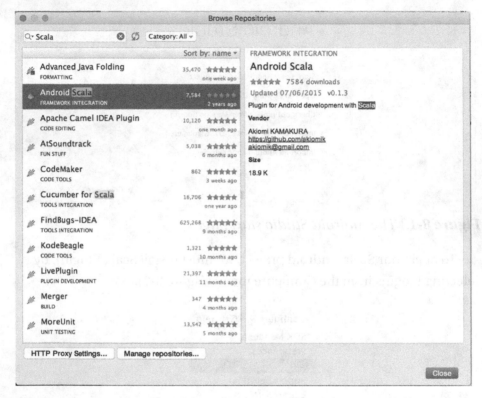

Figure 8-3. *Selection of the Android Scala plug-in*

Install the plug-in and then restart the program. This installs Scala Plugin on Android Studio. We are now ready to create our first Android project.

To create an application, from the start page, select the link *Start new Android Studio Project*. This shows the steps involved in creating the project. First, we must indicate the name of the project and the package (Figure 8-4).

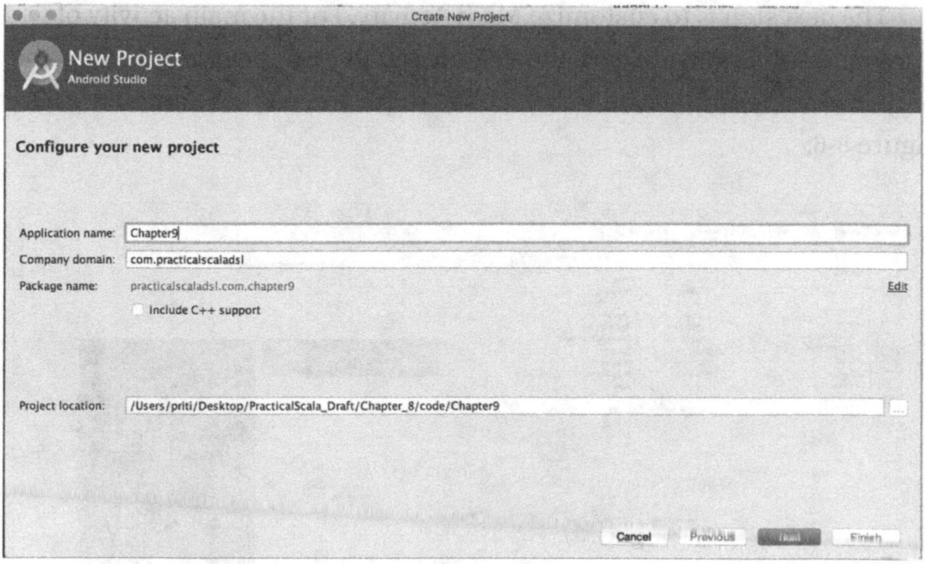

Figure 8-4. Create the new Android Project

Click Next and select the target Android Device. Select the device and click Next. The following screen shows the kind of basic project we want create. Select Basic Activity (Figure 8-5).

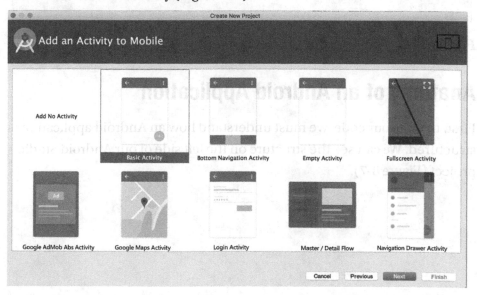

Figure 8-5. Activity mobile selection

The next step is to customize Main Activity. For the main activity of our application, we can leave the default details and click Next. Finally, the project is ready, and, if you follow all the steps, you will see something like Figure 8-6.

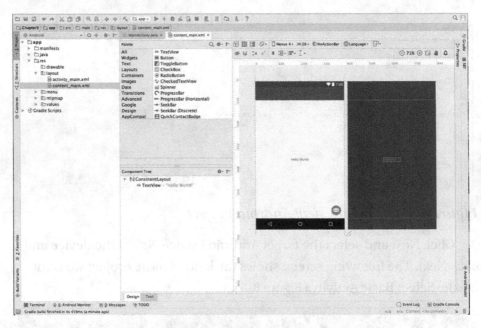

Figure 8-6. *The Android project is ready*

Anatomy of an Android Application

First, to write our code, we must understand how an Android application is structured. We can see the structure on the left side of our Android Studio project (Figure 8-7).

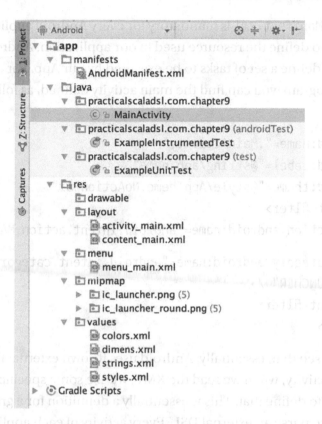

Figure 8-7. *The Android application anatomy*

We can identify three main folders.

- manifests This folder contains AndroidManifest.xml. This file provides the essential information about the application.

- java: This folder contains all Java code.. Android is primary developed in Java. In our case, the Scala files are as well.

- res: This folder contains all no-code files necessary for the application. Here we can find XML files, UI, graphics files, etc.

AndroidManifest.xml is mandatory for every Android application and is used to define the resource used in our application. Android uses Activity to define a set of tasks to be executed by our App. For example, in our basic program, you can find the main activity defined, as follows:

```
<activity
    android:name=".MainActivity"
    android:label="@string/app_name"
    android:theme="@style/AppTheme.NoActionBar">
    <intent-filter>
        <action android:name="android.intent.action.MAIN" />

        <category android:name="android.intent.category.
        LAUNCHER" />
    </intent-filter>
</activity>
```

You can see that, essentially, Android uses its own external DSL. To define the activity, when we read the XML, we see some specific work and action used to define that. This is essentially a definition for a grammar with which to parse an external DSL. Every activity of each application is unique to the purpose of the task. All activity extends the Activity class. This is a building block for every Android application.

The Activity class derives from the Context class. In Android, an activity is essentially a window. From what we see in the application, Context is the central command center for an Android application. Most application functionality can be accessed directly using the Context class. This is essentially an abstract class. This class allows access to all the resources for the application, for example, configuration files, etc. From this class, we can derive all other classes for the operating system.

Our First Scala-Android Application

As of now, to create our Scala Android application, we can call the application `PracticalScalaDSL`. This is because the previous project cannot be an empty project. For a better understanding of the process, it is preferable to start from an empty project. To do that, we start Android Studio and begin a new empty project (Figure 8-8).

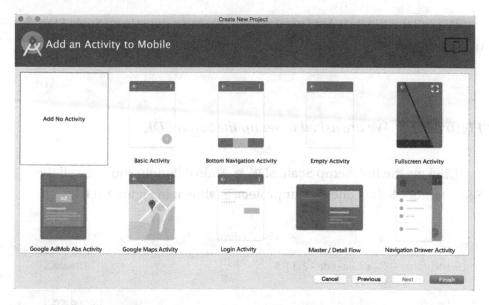

Figure 8-8. *Creating a new project with no activity*

Having created an empty Android project, we can use this project to start to add our Scala class and develop our Scala Android application.

What we need to do first is create a Main window to show a simple "Hello World." In this way, we can see how to use Scala to write our Android application. To do this, we right-click the folder `practicalscaladsl.com.practicalscaladsl` and select the new file, as shown in Figure 8-9.

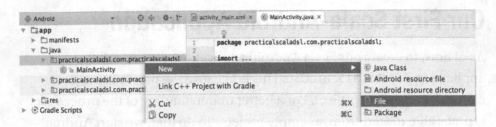

Figure 8-9. *Creating a new file*

We call the file `MainActivity.scala`, because there is no Scala SDK set up. The editor asks us to set up one, as shown in Figure 8-10.

Figure 8-10. *We are asked to set up the Scala SDK*

Clicking the link Setup Scala SDK ➤ AndroidStudio shows us all the Scala editors. Select one for our project, as shown in Figure 8-11.

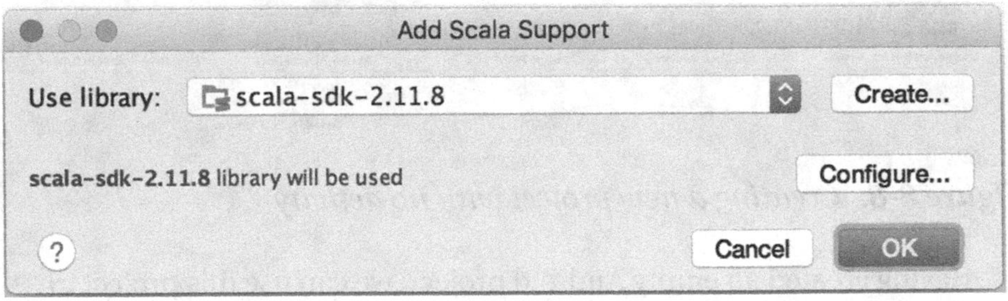

Figure 8-11. *Adding Scala support*

The first code we wrote is the code to create the main windows. The code is very simple and looks like the following:

```
package practicalscaladsl.com.chapter_8

import android.app.Activity
import android.os.Bundle
```

```
class MainActivity extends Activity {
  override def onCreate(savedInstanceState: Bundle) {
    super.onCreate(savedInstanceState)
    setContentView(R.layout.main_layout)
  }
}
```

The code is very simple and easy. We extend the Activity class and override the function onCreate. With this method, we call our layout, in our case, activity_main.xml.

The layout is essentially a resource in Android. We can define the layout in the res package. It is a simple .xml file. This file is created in the folder res, under the foldor layout, as shown in Figure 8-12.

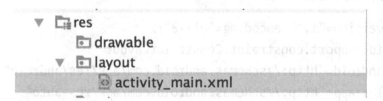

Figure 8-12. *The folder layout*

The content of this file is very simple.

```
<?xml version="1.0" encoding="utf-8"?>
<LinearLayout xmlns:android="http://schemas.android.com/apk/
res/android"
    android:orientation="vertical" android:layout_width="match_
    parent"
    android:layout_height="match_parent">
//This code is used to define a TextView, is essentially a view
with a text the resource we define is basically the kind of
layout, how we want the text and the text itself
```

```
    <TextView
        android:id="@+id/textView"
        android:layout_width="match_parent"
        android:layout_height="wrap_content"
        android:text="Hello Scala" />
</LinearLayout>
```

This simple file creates the layout. In our case, we add a simple TextView, an Android component to show text, and define some property of that.

An Android application defines the Context for calling the other resources, so we must create another resource file to define that. In this case, in the same folder, we create another file, called content_main. The content of the file follows:

```
<?xml version="1.0" encoding="utf-8"?>
<android.support.constraint.ConstraintLayout
xmlns:android="http://schemas.android.com/apk/res/android"
    xmlns:app="http://schemas.android.com/apk/res-auto"
    xmlns:tools="http://schemas.android.com/tools"
    android:layout_width="match_parent"
    android:layout_height="match_parent"
    app:layout_behavior="@string/appbar_scrolling_view_
    behavior"
    tools:context="practicalscaladsl.com.chapter_8.Main
    Activity"
    tools:showIn="@layout/activity_main">

    <TextView
        android:layout_width="wrap_content"
        android:layout_height="wrap_content"
        android:text="Hello World!"
        app:layout_constraintBottom_toBottomOf="parent"
        app:layout_constraintLeft_toLeftOf="parent"
```

```
        app:layout_constraintRight_toRightOf="parent"
        app:layout_constraintTop_toTopOf="parent" />
```

```
</android.support.constraint.ConstraintLayout>
```

This file defines the resources we can use in our Android app. These are the basics for starting the application. What we want to do now is start the code. To do this, we just click the Run button on Android Studio, as shown in Figure 8-13.

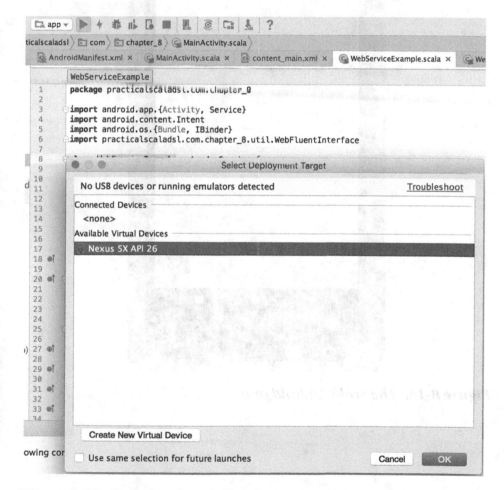

Figure 8-13. *Running the application*

Select the device we have, and start the code. You will see something like Figure 8-14.

Figure 8-14. *The Scala Android app*

We now have defined our layout, and we can see how Android uses an external DSL to define the resources. But now it's time to create our DSL. Our DSL will be used to create a service application, a back-end type of application used to connect with a web service, and get some data. In our case, we create an internal DSL, to create a *service*, another piece of software that we can define in our Android app.

Creating Services in Android

An Android app is not created only with a user interface. An important part of the application is defined by the service. An Android service is like a back-end component for a web application. It doesn't have any interface; it works in the background; and it doesn't have any particular interaction with the user.

We can define different kinds of services. For example, we can define services for the following:

- *Check mail*: We can have a service working in the background to check new mail received and show that in the interface.

- *Check our social network*: We can have a service dedicated to checking our social networks, for example, Facebook, Twitter, LinkedIn, and show a notification in our interface.

These are just two examples of services we can use every day in our mobile phones. Our service need only check a web service and show some updates. For now, we will concentrate on creating the DSL necessary to connect to that.

From a developer's point of view, the creation of a service is relatively simple. We extend the class android.app.Service and then write the code for the service. In our case, the service calls our DSL, via a *fluent API*, to build our action from component parts. What we do is essentially make a call to an external web service to get some result and draw it to the Android application.

```scala
package practicalscaladsl.com.chapter_8

import android.app.{Activity, Service}
import android.content.Intent
import android.os.{Bundle, IBinder}

class WebServiceExample extends Service {

  val mStartMode:Int

  var mBinder:IBinder

  val mAllowRebind:Boolean

  override def onCreate():Unit

  override def onStartCommand(intent:Intent, flags:Int,
  startId:Int):Int = return mStartMode

  override def onBind(intent:Intent):IBinder = return mBinder

  override def onUnbind(intent:Intent):Boolean = return
  mAllowRebind

  override def onRebind(intent:Intent)

  override def onDestroy():Unit
}
```

Our code extends the class Service. This class defines some interface we need to override when we create our method. You'll see more about the method when we integrate our code. We start now to create our DSL to call the service. A service is a component started in the background of our Android application. This class is used when, for example, the application must connect to a network or must execute some background operations. The service starts when an application calls the operation serviceStart. When this is started, the service works in the background and continues to work, even if the application is destroyed. To stop the service, we must close it via the code. To stop the code, we must call the stopService method.

Defining Our DSLs

As we know, a DSL is used to improve communication and allow a developer to better define the interface and the method used to create an API. So, we start with some method we can use for the fluent API. The first step is to define the common dictionary and the action we want solve (Table 8-1).

Table 8-1. *The Basic Definition of Our DSL*

Method	Definition
Connect	Execute the connection on the web service
Find(string Name)	Find a user using the web service
Add(string Name)	Add a new user to the system

We define three simple actions for our service. We don't really need to add more action to show how to create the DSL. Our goal is to show how we can integrate the DSL in Android development.

We start now to create our DSL, using the fluent API interface. This kind of method is used to create a chain of calls that we can read like English. So, we now create the code for the interface and see that it looks like the following:

```
package practicalscaladsl.com.chapter_8.util

import java.util

import sun.net.www.http.HttpClient

class WebFluentInterface {
  private var entity=""
  private var httpResponse= ""
  private var httpClient=""
```

```scala
private var webService = ""

case class Username(username:String)

def Connect(webservice:String):Unit ={
  this.webService= webservice
  this
}

def Find(username:String):Unit ={
  httpClient = new DefaultHttpClient()
  httpResponse = httpClient.execute(new HttpGet(webservice))
  entity = httpResponse.getEntity()
  this
}

def add(username:String):Unit = {

  val user = new Username(username)
  val userJson = new Gson().toJson(user)

  val post = new HttpPost(this.webService)
  val nameValuePairs = new util.ArrayList[NameValuePair]()
  nameValuePairs.add(new BasicNameValuePair("JSON",
  userJson))
  post.setEntity(new UrlEncodedFormEntity(nameValuePairs))

  val client = new DefaultHttpClient
  val response = client.execute(post)
  println("--- HEADERS ---")
  response.getAllHeaders.foreach(arg => println(arg))
  this
 }

}
```

The code is a simple fluent API call. We have the three methods we can use to call the web service and post the data. The important part of the code is how we can use it in Android.

We can do that by improving the Service class we just wrote, as follows:

```
package practicalscaladsl.com.chapter_8

import android.app.{Activity, Service}
import android.content.Intent
import android.os.{Bundle, IBinder}
import practicalscaladsl.com.chapter_8.util.WebFluentInterface

class WebServiceExample extends Service {

  val mStartMode:Int

  var mBinder:IBinder

  val mAllowRebind:Boolean

  val webFluentInterface:WebFluentInterface

  override def onCreate():Unit

  override def onStartCommand(itent:Intent, flags:Int,
  startId:Int):Int = {
    webFluentInterface.
      Connect("http://localhost:8080/add").
      Add("Test")
    return mStartMode
  }
```

```
override def onBind(intent:Intent):IBinder = return mBinder

override def onUnbind(intent:Intent):Boolean = return
mAllowRebind

override def onRebind(intent:Intent)

override def onDestroy():Unit
}
```

You can see that we created the call for the method in the method
onStartCommand. This creates the call necessary to add a new user in
the web service. This is the simplest way to create a connection from the
Android app and our DSL.

Conclusion

Mobile development is a hot prospect at the moment. In this chapter,
we've just scratched its surface. You've seen how to create an Android
project and learned the basics of Android development. Of course, this is
merely a start.

For a good description of mobile development, another book is
probably required. We will now use Scala instead of Java and, at the same
time, see how we can use DSLs to define some utility class for the service.
Using a DSL in our development is just a new way of working. We don't
need to think of the DSL as some strange technique, but only as a simple
way of writing our code.

In the next chapter, we see other uses of DSLs and how simply they can
be used in our daily work.

CHAPTER 9

Forex Trading System

So far, we've used DSLs in different areas. What you'll see now is how to create a Forex (foreign-exchange) trading system. Today, more and more people are interested in investment, and an increasing number of developers work in finance.

In this chapter, you will see how to use Scala and DSLs to create a complete library for Forex trading. You will also see how DSLs make using the system simple.

What Is a Forex Trading System?

A Forex trading system is a tool created to buy and sell in the Forex market. The system is based on a set of rules used to buy and sell currency. A Forex trading system usually is based on a set of signals. By signal is meant some specific indicator and value we identify and use that is derived from technical analysis.

Every system can be configured to better manage the system. We can tell the system how to open and close a position and define the kinds of instruments we want to use for technical analysis.

In Forex, there are some specific terms used commonly to define a position and identify a gain or loss in the market. To start to create our system, we must define the words and their meanings. This becomes our new common dictionary for defining the method and syntax of our DSL (Table 9-1).

© Pierluigi Riti 2018
P. Riti, *Practical Scala DSLs*, https://doi.org/10.1007/978-1-4842-3036-7_9

Table 9-1. *Dictionary of Items Used in Our Forex Trading System*

Term	Description
PIP	Price interest point. This is indicated by the last digit in the rate, which represents the cost of every point that changes in value. For example, EUR/USD 1 point = 0.0001 is used to calculate the standard rate, which rises or falls with the change in the value of 1 point. A PIP measures the amount of change in the exchange rate for a currency pair. For currency pairs displayed to four decimal places, one pip is equal to 0.0001. Yen-based currency pairs are an exception and are displayed to only two decimal places (0.01).
BID	Price of the demand; the price you sell for
ASK	Price of the offer; the price you buy for
CARRY TRADE	Holding a position with a positive overnight interest return, in hope of gaining profits, without closing the position; just for the central banks' interest rate differences
BANK RATE	The percentage rate at which the central bank of a country lends money to the country's commercial banks
COMMISSION	Broker commissions for operation handling
CURRENCY PAIRS	The duo of currencies to buy/sell, for example, EUR/USD (euro/US dollar) or EUR/GBP (euro/Great British pound)
RATE	The agreed exchange rate between two currencies. For example, the value of the EUR/USD for a specific day being 1.500
PRINCIPAL AMOUNT	Called sometimes "face" or "nominal," the amount of currency involved in the deal
TIME FRAME	The time of a current operation

(continued)

Table 9-1. (*continued*)

Term	Description
DAY TRADING	Position on trading open and close on the same day
LEVERAGE	The money invested when starting a new position. For example, a leverage with a value of 1,000 with 100 dollars invested translates into a real investment of 1000 × 100 = 1,000,000 dollars. Leverage is important for ascribing a value to a PIP.
PROFIT	Positive amount of money gained after closing the position
LOSS	The money lost in an already closed position
STOP LOSS	The amount of PIP or money lost at the close of a position
TAKE PROFIT	The amount of PIP or money gained at the close of a position
STANDARD ACCOUNT	Account position with $100,000
MINI ACCOUNT	Account position with $10,000
MICRO ACCOUNT	Account position with $1,000

Using this table, we can now define the problem and design our DSL.

Designing the DSL System

With the common dictionary defined, we can begin to design the system and see what we need to implement it. The first step in designing the system is to identify the rules we want to use for it. As we know that a DSL can be used to implement a system using calls, similar to plain English, what we do now is define these rules and implement them.

First, to design the system, we must understand how the Forex trading market works. The Forex trading market primarily buys and sells currency. This is done using specific platforms that allows clients to buy currency pairs, for example EUR/USD (euros/US dollars). A gain or loss is the difference in the number of PIP from when we started to hold a position and when we closed that position.

We can define a stop loss or take a profit to close the position when we have gained or lost a certain number of PIP. When we place an order in a Forex trading system, it looks like the following:

> BUY EUR/USD $1,000 with a LEVERAGE of 10, with
> a TAKE PROFIT of 10 PIP and a STOP LOSS of 10 PIP

With the rules we can use to describe our system in place, we can place an order to buy a currency pair, define a leverage and a stop loss, and the take a profit. Using a command, we can define our system rules and, based on that, define our system.

The rules we want to implement in our system are simple.

- The system must be allowed to buy currency.

- The system must be allowed to sell currency.

- The system must be able to set a stop loss.

- The system must be able to set a profit.

- The system must be able to define the currency pair.

- The system must be able to define a leverage.

These defined rules allow the system to create exactly the same line we defined previously. What we need to do now is define the object involved in the DSL.

We can start now to write the code we need to define the system. The first piece of code we need is for implementing the rules. What we require is a set of objects. These objects can be brought together to carry out the rules.

Implementing the System

The first step is to design the object necessary for defining our currency pairs. The first object we can define is the currency. The code for the currency is as follows:

```
trait CurrencyType{
  def pair: String
}
```

What we define with the preceding code is essentially the generic way of defining the currency we use in the system. The scope of the trait is defined by a generic object that we can "specialize" for use in the creation of the currency pair.

The next code we must write is that necessary for defining the currency pair.

```
class CurrencyPair(val accountType:String) extends
CurrencyType{

  override def pair(currency_name:String):String
={ currency_name }

  def PIP(): Double={
    val first_currency=pair("USD")
    val second_currency=pair("EUR")

    var returnPIP:Double=0.0
    if (secondary.toString.equalsIgnoreCase("USD")){
      if (accountType.equalsIgnoreCase("MICRO")){
        returnPIP=0.10
      }
```

```
    else if (accountType.equalsIgnoreCase("MINI")){
      returnPIP=1
    }
    else if (accountType.equalsIgnoreCase("STANDARD")){
      returnPIP=10
    }
  }

  return returnPIP
  }
}
```

The preceding code shows how we can define a `CurrencyPair` and define the PIP we gain, depending on the account. Now you can see that we use the trait class to define the kind of currency pair we want to use in the system.

The `CurrencyPair` class allows us to create the currency pair and to show some features of Scala. The line of code `class CurrencyPair (val accountType:String) extends CurrencyType` shows how trait is used. We can see that this simply extends the class and overrides the method of the trait. This creates the concrete method based on the interface.

The class then takes care of calculating the value of the PIP of each account, depending on the type. By definition, when the secondary currency is the US dollar (USD), we can define the default values of the three types of accounts—micro, mini, and standard—which are $0.10, $1, and $10.

This results from the PIP method, which does nothing but confirm the type of object and then return the value of the PIP.

Improving the Basic Class

Based on the previous code, we can make some improvements. For example, we can create a new class, Account, to remove the if then and create a better code, as follows:

```
trait AccountType{
  def account:Double
}
```

The first improvement we make is to create another trait to define the account type. The account can be of three types: MICRO, MINI, or STANDARD. We can use the new trait extending the class that was written previously. In Scala, it is possible to have multiple inheritance using the word with. Here is the new code.

```
class CurrencyPair(accountType:String) extends CurrencyType
with AccountType{

  override def pair(currency_name:String):String
={ currency_name }

  override def account(account_type:String):Double={
    if (account_type.equalsIgnoreCase("MICRO")){
      return 0.1
    }else if(account_type.equalsIgnoreCase("MINI")){
      return 1
    }else if(account_type.equalsIgnoreCase("STANDARD")){
      return 10
    }
  }
}
```

```
def PIP(): Double={
  val first_currency=pair("EUR")

  val second_currency=pair("USD")

  val pip=new account("MINI")

  return pip
 }
}
```

Creating the Order

The next step is to create an order. This is essentially the basic operation of the trading system. The system should be able to create an order using the basic parameter, so let's now create the class.

```
class Order(val pair: CurrencyPair){
  def ask(profit:Int,loss:Int ):Unit={
    println("Profit:"+profit)
    println("Loss:"+loss)
    println("PIP:"+pair.PIP)
  }
  def bid(profit:Int,loss:Int):Uint={
    println("Profit:"+profit)
    println("Loss:"+loss)
    println("PIP:"+pair.PIP)
  }
}
```

The class is very simple. It has only two methods: one to buy, ask(), and one to sell, bind(). Both methods accept two parameters, profit and loss.

Now we can see that the name of the method uses the name defined in the dictionary. This is because we want to define a software that can be read like plain English. The next step is to create the code for placing an order. To do this, we have only to create a variable called _order, with a syntax like the following:

```
val _order = new Order(new CurrencyPair("MICRO","EUR","USD")).
ask(10,10)
```

The call uses the fluent style. This is essentially a DSL call, but its syntax is not exactly good for defining that, because one of the core elements of DSLs is how we define the API. The code until now is very basic and somewhat confusing. The API is not very clear, and creating a call with it is not as smooth as we would like. Of course, we can read it like English, but a good DSL should be very simple to read and understand.

So, what we need to do to have a good DSL is first to design a good API. This is not an easy job but is the crucial difference in having a good DSL or not. If we see to the actual DSL, for example, the HTML, or the RubyDSL used in Chef, we can see a clear and simple definition of some APIs. An API with a clear name and documentation helps a developer to write the code. What we need to identify now is why and how to write a good API.

Why It Is Important to Design a Good API

The API is essentially the interface used by the software to communicate with the outside world. Designing a good API is the key to having successful software.

If we design a good API, the API "talks" by itself. If we use a good name to define it, or a good interface, it's easily understandable and simple to use. Designing a good API requires rules and experience, so let's identify some rules that we can use when we have to design our API.

- Use a simple and clear name. The name must be understandable to the people using the API. So, if the API is for Forex, the name of the method must be something related.

- Every API must have a specific version. Versioning is the developers' check if the software is compatible or not. Versioning the API can better communicate to the developer which features are available and which are not.

- The API must have good documentation. Good documentation creates good APIs. Having good documentation allows the developer who consumes the API to understand clearly what the API can or can't do. Spending time to create good documentation is a wise investment.

These three pillars are essentially the basics for designing and maintaining a good API. When we write a DSL, we essentially create a set of APIs to solve a specific problem. By adhering to these three pillars, we can rewrite the software we have created until now and make it more readable and more DSL-efficient.

The way to use these three pillars is connected to the user experience and having a good plan. The first step we can take to implement the pillars is planning the API. Using the common dictionary provides a good start for planning the name of the API. Essentially, every API must be one functionality of the system. In our case, we must have an API like PIP, BID, ASK, etc.

Using these names helps us to respect another pillar: the documentation. We can use the common dictionary for documentation. Because we have the same name for the API we use in the common dictionary, we can use it for documenting the API. In essence, the system must respond with a specific functionality described in the common dictionary, and to use the API, this is enough.

The last consideration we must keep in mind is versioning. When we create an API, we must understand that we can have different versions of the same API. This can be managed, for example, by creating a different end point or by slightly changing a name, for example, change that of the package.

Based on my experience, the best approach is to use the package to manage the versioning. This is because every developer can easily identify what he/she needs and then import the correct package for the software. Versioning allows us to have different versions of the software but one common response. Versioning is normally used to resolve an issue or. make improvements to software.

Based on that, we can identify the next steps to improve our code. What we have to do is create a version of our API and, of course, improve the interface for it, because we want to upgrade our DSL to the next level. When we version an API, we essentially create a different end point for it. To do this, we create a new package. For example, if we create a structure `practicalscaladsl/v1/api`, a second version would be `practicalscaladsl/v2/api`.

Because we change the package, we create two different versions for the code. This is used, for example, when we must update the version of the software, such as by adding some functionality, but we want to maintain the old API.

Designing the New DSL API

To improve the quality of the first version of the DSL code that we started with, and respecting the design pillars we just defined, we must update the code. We define a version of the code. This helps to manage the improvement and creates the API to respect the common dictionary we have defined.

The first step in creating a good API is to define a package. So, the first modification that we make to the code is the definition of the package. In Scala, we can define a package with the following code:

```
package com{
  package practicalscala{
    package v1{
      class TradingSystem{
        ......
      }
    }
  }
}
```

In Scala, we define a package simply by using the reserved word package, followed by the name of package. In our code, for example, we defined a package com.practicalscala.v1. When we create a package in Scala, it is not mandatory for the language to create the folder structure of the package. In Java, for example, it is mandatory to create the same package structure.

We can now start to rewrite the class TradingSystem. What we want to do first is define the pair of currencies, so let's start to create the method pair to do that.

```
package com {
  package practicalscala {
    package v1 {
      class TradingSystem {
        protected var _pair: String = ""

        def pair(first: String, second: String): this.type = {
          this._pair = s"$first/$second"
          this
        }
```

```
    def execute() ={
      println(_pair)
    }
  }
 }
}
}
```

You can see that the method pair has been added to the class
TradingSystem. The method only creates the pair and nothing more, but
this gives us an idea of how we can use the package for versioning. To
call the class, we must first import the class TradingSystem. Of course,
because we still use the fluent API, we must execute a method to return
the value calculated by the class. An interesting feature of the preceding
code is the *string interpolation*. In Scala, the char s before a string tells the
interpreter to interpolate it. This is a new feature added in Scala 2.10. With
the string interpolation, the developer can use variables processed by
Scala, and their result, to build a string. This is useful when, for example,
we want the string to change according to the value of some variable's or
operation's result. We can also use operations, in this case the syntax ${
}, to define the operation. In our case, we use this functionality to create
the currency pair. The code s"$first/$second" interpolates the string at
runtime and changes the variables first and second with the parameter
for the method.

The _pair variable is shared in the class. Using a class variable, in this
case, is protected. This means that no method outside the package can
be used by the variable. This is fine for us, because the package essentially
contains only the method we want to expose for our DSL. So, let's consume
this first version of the API and see the result.

Consuming the First API

Having written the first API, it is now time to consume it. The main method is

```scala
import com.practicalscala.v1._

object TestMain{
  def main(args:Array[String]):Unit ={
    val _pair = new TradingSystem()
    println(_pair.pair("USD","EUR").execute())
  }
}
```

The code is quite simple. To import the API, we use this line of code: `import com.practicalscala.v1._`. There is no significant difference in the Java syntax, only that when we want to import all classes of a package in Java, we use the * (asterisk). In Scala, we use the _ (underscore). The rest is very simple. We create the class `TradingSystem` and call the `pair` method. This returns to us the value of the currency pair. If we execute the code, we have a result like the following:

USD/EUR

The next step that we need to take is to improve the API and define the function for the Forex trading system. We continue to improve the API with the other method and create the method chain we must use to place an order in bid or ask.

Improving the API

The API we have designed for the trading system is very basic. We must add more operations to the system. The first adjustment we must make is to define the kind of account we want. This is used to calculate the value of the PIP. The code for that is

```
def account(_type:String):this.type = {
  this._account_value = (_type: @switch) match {
    case "MICRO" => 0.1
    case "MINI" => 1
    case "STANDARD" => 10
  }
  this
}
```

The code sets the value of _account_value. This is done by using the notation @switch. This changes how we use pattern matching. For that, we have to import the package scala.annotation.switch. This annotation compiles the code in a tableswitch or a lookupswitch. This offers better performance, because the compiler internally translates the switch in a branch table instead of a decision tree.

We can see in the code that the annotation @switch allows us to create a very compact decision code, connected to a variable. What we want is to match the type of the account with any difference in the PIP. The PIP is used to calculate the profit/loss resulting from every transaction.

We can now rewrite the main method in the following way:

```
object TestMain{
  def main(args:Array[String]):Unit ={
    val _pair = new TradingSystem()
    println(_pair.pair("USD","EUR").account("MINI").execute())
  }
}
```

We can see that we have a better fluency in API for now. Next, we define an account, a pair, and, finally, execute. If we execute now, we get the following result:

```
USD/EUR
PIP Value:1.0
```

The execution returns the pair and the PIP value. It is now time to add more complexity to our system.

Adding the Last Functionality

The Forex trading system requires additional functionality to be complete, so let's start to add more. The first functions to add functionality to, such as stop loss or take profit, define the capital to be invested.

The first function we add is to take profits. The code for that is

```
def take_profit(pip:Int):this.type ={
  this._pip_profit = pip
  this._max_capital_profit =(this._capital+(this._pip_value * pip))
  this
}
```

The take_profit function has the parameter pip. This indicates the number of PIP we can accept to lose before closing the position. Internally, the function defines the value max_capital_profit. This is used to calculate the new capital and close the position.

Note The function uses this.type to define the return type. This is used in Scala to return the type of method. Because we still have a fluent API pattern, we must be clear about what type we must return. Using this.type allows the function to return the type at runtime, without specifying the type of return first. This is useful when we build a DSL, in particular, when we want functionality that can have more than one type of return.

The other function we can add is `stop_loss`. This is used to close the position when it loses too much PIP. The function looks like this:

```
def stop_loss(pip:Int):this.type  ={
  this._pip_lost = pip
  this._max_capital_lost = (this._capital-(this._pip_value * pip))
  this
}
```

We can see that the function is similar to `take_profit`. At the end, both have the same function: they continue to add functionality to the system. The end of the code looks like this:

```
import scala.annotation.switch
import scala.math.BigDecimal

package com {
  package practicalscala {
    package v1 {
      class TradingSystem {
        protected var _pair: String = ""
        protected var _pip_value: BigDecimal = 0.0
        protected var _pip_profit:Int = 0
        protected var _pip_lost:Int = 0
        protected var _start_position:BigDecimal =0.0
        protected var _actual_value:BigDecimal = 0.0
        protected var _capital:BigDecimal = 0
        protected var _max_capital_lost:BigDecimal = 0
        protected var _max_capital_profit:BigDecimal =0

        def pair(first: String, second: String): this.type  = {
          this._pair = s"$first/$second"
          this
        }
```

```
def account(_type:String):this.type = {
  this._pip_value = (_type: @switch) match {
    case "MICRO" => 0.1
    case "MINI" => 1
    case "STANDARD" => 10
  }
  this
}

def take_profit(pip:Int):this.type ={
  this._pip_profit = pip
  this._max_capital_profit =(this._capital+(this._pip_
  value * pip))
  this
}

def stop_loss(pip:Int):this.type ={
  this._pip_lost = pip
  this._max_capital_lost = (this._capital-(this._pip_
  value * pip))
  this
}

def start_position(start_value:Double):this.type ={
  this._start_position=start_value
  this
}

def actual_position(actual_value:Double):this.type ={
  this._actual_value=actual_value
  this
}
```

```scala
    def capital(investment:Int):this.type ={
      this._capital=investment
      this
    }

    def execute() ={
      val _gain=(this._actual_value - this._start_position)
      val _check_profit =((_gain * this._pip_value) + _
      capital)

      if(_check_profit > _max_capital_profit){
        println("Max Profit gain")
      }else if(_check_profit > _max_capital_lost){
        println("Stop loss gain")
      }
      println("PIP gained:"+_gain)
      println("Actual Capital:"+_check_profit)
    }
  }
 }
}
}
```

You can see that BigDecimal has been imported. This is used in Scala to define the currency type. Because a currency can have more decimal numbers, BigDecimal helps to define that. The function that has changed most is execute. This essentially is the core of the system. This calculates the gain and checks the profit. If the value is as specified, we close the position, whether there is a gain or loss.

Now let's see how we can use the Forex trading system to set a position that takes a profit and stops a loss.

```scala
import com.practicalscala.v1._

object TestMain{
  def main(args:Array[String]):Unit ={
    val _pair = new TradingSystem()
    println(_pair.pair("USD","EUR")
      .account("MINI")
        .start_position(1.0455)
        .actual_position(1.0554)
        .stop_loss(10)
        .take_profit(10)
        .capital(10000)
        .execute())

    println(_pair.pair("USD","EUR")
      .account("MINI")
        .start_position(1.0455)
        .actual_position(1.0354)
        .stop_loss(10)
        .take_profit(10)
        .capital(10000)
        .execute())
  }
}
```

We create a chain to call the method. We specify the currency pair, the kind of account, the start position, the value at which we buy the currency, the actual position, the position updated, the stop loss and the take profit, and, finally, the capital.

At the end, we call execute, to determine whether we have as a result of the position a gain or loss. Of course, it is best to connect the system with a real-time Forex and let it change the value. In this case, we can use the system for real.

When we execute the system, we have a result such as the following:

```
Max Profit gain
PIP gained:0.0099
Actual Capital:10000.0099

Stop loss gain
PIP gained:-0.0101
Actual Capital:9999.9899
```

The system calculates the PIP gained or lost and updates the capital. Then, based on the PIP, it decides what is needed to close the position.

Conclusion

You have now seen how to use a DSL to create a trading system. This is not complex; we only need to re-think how we work every day.

The big advantage of using a DSL is how easily it reads the code and how simple it is to understand. Another small advantage is the complexity of the function. Because we define a method chain, we can write very simple functions that can be connected. This allows us to write a simple functionality that we can connect with others to solve big problems, write simple functions, and simplify the maintenance of the code itself. It is always easier to maintain a small function than one with more than one hundred lines of code.

In this chapter, you discovered additional Scala functionality, such as the switch notation and this.type, both of which allow us to write simple and efficient code, which, of course, is crucial when we want write a good DSL.

In the next chapter, I will discuss another important topic: games. You will see how to build a video game using a DSL.

CHAPTER 10

Game Development

Games are as old as humankind and continue to be important in contemporary societies. The first electronic game was Pong. A two-dimensional sports game, it essentially involved only a ball moving from the left side of the screen and two bars trying to stop the ball from scoring points. The first iteration of an electronic game dates from 1966.

Since 1966, the game industry has evolved, and now we can find games with sophisticated graphics and gameplay. Now, it is possible even to find games with 3D graphics on a mobile phone. In this chapter, you will see how to begin to create a simple game engine with Scala. We will create a set of APIs using a DSL. In this way, we can create a call for our game in a simple, understandable way.

Game Team Structure

Working with a DSL means that we create software that can be "read" and understood not only by technical folks. To do that, we must know the domain of the problem.

The first step in understanding a domain is to know the structure and the actor involved in our software development. So, in our case, the first step is to understand a team game structure. This is important when it comes to designing and defining our DSL. We try now to define the different teams and see how they interact with each other.

© Pierluigi Riti 2018
P. Riti, *Practical Scala DSLs*, https://doi.org/10.1007/978-1-4842-3036-7_10

Engineering Team

The engineering team is responsible for all the engineering work. This means developing the game, designing the tools necessary for the game, and maintaining the build.

Engineers can be divided into two basic categories: *runtime* engineers, or game engineers, the people responsible for developing the game engine itself, and *tools* engineers, those responsible for developing the sets of tools to be used in the engine, or by other engineers, to develop the game.

Generally, these engineering categories also have subcategories. For example, there are also AI engineers, who specialize in defining artificial intelligence (AI), or graphic engineers, specialists in the graphic interfaces. In recent years, other engineering specialties related to games have emerged, such as *server* engineers. These engineers specialize in developing the server side of the game. For more and more games, particularly mobile games, the server is a big part of the engine driving the game. It is used in cooperation with the client to manage the game.

All the engineers mentioned work together to build a game. Of course, every type of engineer talks a specific language directly connected to the type of job he or she does. In the games field creating a good DSL can be crucial for defining and promoting good communication across a team. Some companies employ a technical director, who is responsible for managing one or more projects, coordinating the development, and, sometimes, managing communication across the team. In this context, having a good common dictionary for designing the DSL can help the technical director to manage that communication and do a better job.

Like any other software company, some studios have a chief technical officer (CTO). This is a higher-level engineer and is essentially an executive position. The CTO provides technical direction to all the engineers in a company.

Artist Team

The artist is another important person necessary for building a good video game. Artists, like the engineers, can be divided into several different categories. The basic divisions are as follows:

- *3D artists*: These artists work exclusively with 3D, for example, modeling the environment and characters in a game.

- *Environment artists*: The artists are responsible for designing the environment of the game.

- *Light artists*: Artists specializing in the lighting design for a game

- *Concept artists*: These artists are responsible for designing new games or developing new concepts for older ones.

- *Animators*: Artists responsible for animating 3D models and giving "life" to game characters

- *Texture artists*: In game design, a model should be very easy, with a very low poly (having the fewest possible polygons in a polygon mesh). Improvement of the texture in the final design is accomplished by texture artists. These artists design textures for the entire game.

These are only a few varieties of artists. Although there are a lot of different artists, generally one works with one of those mentioned. Some other artists are relegated to only one phase of the development of a game and are never in direct contact with an engineer. However, to talk to each other, roles and responsibilities must be defined.

Other Actors Involved

Realizing a video game requires teamwork. Figures assuming roles other than the technical ones I have described are also essential to managing the development life cycle.

Producer

The producer is the person responsible for managing the nontechnical aspects of the development, managing tasks, human resources, and helping to remove obstacles in the development.

Marketing and Customer Service

Crucial aspects of a game's release are marketing and customer service, particularly for modern game development for mobile or MMOs (massively multiplayer online games) to maintain a correct approach to users, and to help the team driving changes in a game to execute their goals. At the same time, marketing is responsible for the advertising campaign and promoting the sale of a game.

Game Designer

The game designer is responsible for the design of the game. Every game has one or more game designers responsible for defining all the logic and the story for the game. This is an artist role and is crucial for defining a good story. A good game design is like a good direction in a film. A good director makes a good film. The same is true for a game.

Definition of a Game Engine

A "game engine" is software used to create a video game. The first time the term was used was for the game Doom, in themid-1990s. The game is a first-person shooter, or FPS, type, wherein the hero must shoot everything that moves around the screen.

184

The novelty of Doom is the perfect division of the different areas of the game. The AI is defined in one part and the 3D graphic programming in another. This separation between areas allowed the developer to create an "engine," part of the software that could be reused for another game.

For example, the area of the code to calculate the physics can be reused. This separation created the first game engine. Through the years, many other engines were born; for example, Unity 3D and Unreal. All these engines have in common the possibility of creating a game using the common library of the engine. For example, the AI has some specific paradigm ready to define the objects and the interactions among them.

Over the years, game engines have evolved and are now used for specific game genres. Newer engines for FPS, such as Unreal, or for generic 3D purposes, such as Unity 3D, have specific characteristics and, sometimes, a specific language. This means that a developer must change engines frequently, making it necessary to re-learn the basic syntax.

The specific game engines for platform or racing games, for example, define some specific rules for the physics and interaction between the different objects in the game. This creates the need for different libraries. Of course, all the engines have some specific characteristics in common, such as the control, but each engine is essentially different.

We can summarize the basic functionality of a game engine as follows:

- Renders the object on the screen; can be 2D or 3D

- Manages the AI for interactions between objects

- Allows use of the control to move the object(s)

- Includes some basic physics laws for the game

These are some generic and minimal guidelines. Every game engine starts with these simple rules, with which we can define our game engine.

Designing Our New DSL Game Engine

So far, I have described what a game engine is and what common functionalities it must have. First, we want a game engine with a good UI, so we must define this feature. Second, we want to define the control necessary to move the object(s) around the screen. Finally, we want to have some generic feature connected to the AI of the game. With these requirements in mind, let's start to define some code.

The first functionality we must define is the game life cycle. This is essentially the entire cycle of a game. It can vary, depending on the game, but generally, there are some steps to be taken in every single game.

The life cycle is independent of the story. For example, a game can have a total gameplay of 20 hours. The gameplay is the total time required to finish the game, and this is strictly connected to the story. The life cycle indicates the state in which the player(s) can be during the execution of the gameplay.

Normally, we have a status start, which indicates when the game begins; pause, used when we include a pause in the action of the game; resume, used when we want to resume a game, for example, after when we have paused the game; and end, for example, when a player is dead.

By adding these basic statuses, we can include other statuses specific to the game. For example, we can have a status "menu," which can be used in some games to enter a status when the game menu is shown. For now, we take care only of the basic status.

To define the status, we create a specific class. This class is used to define all the statuses in the game. When we think about software for a game, essentially, we consider a complex *state machine*. Every state of the machine can have within it more complex states. This is basically the core of our game. We can define some basic states, as follows:

- Start

- Pause

- Resume

- End

186

All these states are basically conditions for managing the game. Every game has a starting point, used to manage the other interactions in the game. The first class we must write is the game core to manage status.

```
package ch10

trait StateMachine {

    def start(): Unit

    def resume(): Unit

    def pause(): Unit

    def end(): Unit
}
```

StateMachine is a Scala trait. A trait is a kind of interface in Scala. A trait is similar to the Java interface. The main difference between a trait and a Java interface is that the trait can be initialized and doesn't accept parameters.

Classes can extend the trait and use it to define the common method defined in the trait. In our case, this trait defines the basics of our game engine. This trait defines the basic action of our state machine.

A game has an interface and sound, so we must define five macro areas for building our engine, as follows:

- Graphic

- Audio

- System

- Windows

- Input

We must define all these classes for use in the game engine. For example, the graphics class can be used to define a 2D or 3D game. In our case, we will use a 2D graphic engine. The next step is to define the main class for the game.

Defining the Generic Component

What we must do now is define the basic component for the game engine. First, we define the audio.

```scala
package ch10

trait Audio {

  abstract class Sound {

    type PlaySound

    def play(volume: Float): PlaySound

    def play(): PlaySound = play(1f)

    def loop(volume: Float): PlaySound
    def loop(): PlaySound = loop(1f)

    def pause(id: PlaySound): Unit
    def resume(id: PlaySound): Unit

    def stop(id: PlaySound): Unit

    def dispose(): Unit

  }
  type SoundType <: Sound

  def loadSoundFromSource(path: String): SoundType

  abstract class Music {
    def play(): Unit
    def pause(): Unit

    def stop(): Unit

    def setVolume(volume: Float): Unit
```

```
    def setLooping(isLooping: Boolean): Unit

    def dispose(): Unit
  }
  type MusicType <: Music
  def loadMusicFromSource(path: String): MusicType

}
```

The Audio file contains some traits, used to define the method and the functionality used for managing the music. We can see that the methods are self-explanatory. We can simply read and understand what the method does.

Another class we must define is the class connected with the graphics. To define the graphic component, we add a helper. This is used to maintain some general methods of the class. The code is the following:

```
package ch10

trait GraphicHelper {
  this: Graphic =>

  implicit class UpdateCanvas(canvas: Canvas) {

    def RepeatBitmap(bitmap: Bitmap, x: Int, y: Int, width:
    Int, height: Int): Unit = {
      val imageWidth = bitmap.width
      val imageHeight = bitmap.height

      val columns: Int = width/imageWidth
      val rows: Int = height/imageHeight

      for(i <- 0 until columns) {
        for(j <- 0 until rows) {
          canvas.drawBitmap(bitmap, x+i*imageWidth,
          y+j*imageHeight)
        }
      }
```

```
    val missingWidth = width - columns*imageWidth
    if(missingWidth > 0) {
      for(i <- 0 until rows)
        canvas.drawBitmap(bitmap, x+columns*imageWidth,
        y+i*imageHeight, 0, 0, missingWidth, imageHeight)
    }
    val missingHeight = height - rows*imageHeight
    if(missingHeight > 0) {
      for(i <- 0 until columns)
        canvas.drawBitmap(bitmap, x+i*imageWidth,
        y+rows*imageHeight, 0, 0, imageWidth, missingHeight)
    }

    if(missingWidth > 0 && missingHeight > 0) {
      canvas.drawBitmap(bitmap, columns*imageWidth,
      rows*imageHeight, 0, 0, missingWidth, missingHeight)
    }

  }

  def drawBitmap(region: ImageRegion, x: Int, y: Int): Unit =
{
    canvas.drawBitmap(region.bitmap, x, y, region.x,
    region.y, region.width, region.height)
  }

}

case class ImageRegion(
  val bitmap: Bitmap, val x: Int, val y: Int,
  val width: Int, val height: Int) {
```

```scala
  def this(bitmap: Bitmap) = this(bitmap, 0, 0, bitmap.width,
  bitmap.height)
}

class Animation(
  var frameDuration: Long,
  frames: Array[ImageRegion],
  var playMode: Animation.PlayMode = Animation.Normal
)
{
  def currentFrame(time: Long): ImageRegion = {
  val frameNumber: Int = ((time/frameDuration) % Int.
  MaxValue).toInt

  val frameIndex = playMode match {
    case Animation.Normal =>
      math.min(frames.size - 1, frameNumber)
    case Animation.Reversed =>
      math.max(frames.size - frameNumber - 1, 0)
    case Animation.Loop =>
      frameNumber % frames.size
    case Animation.LoopReversed =>
      frames.length - (frameNumber % frames.size) - 1

    frames(frameIndex)
  }

  def isCompleted(time: Long): Boolean = time > animation
  Duration

  def animationDuration: Long = frames.size*frameDuration
}
object Animation {
```

```
    sealed trait Play

    case object Normal extends Play
    case object Reversed extends Play
    case object Loop extends Play
    case object LoopReversed extends Play
    }
}
```

This code is a little complex, but inside it, we find every single piece of interface we require to manage the graphics of the game. The trait GraphicHelper introduces a new functionality of Scala 2.10, the *implicit class.*

This feature is very helpful, because it helps to define that a class can have a primary constructor available when we create it. This means, for example, that we can use this class to create different types of game objects using different constructors, but we call all with the same type of call.

Note   An implicit class is a new type of class introduced in Scala 2.10. An implicit class is a normal Scala class created with the word `implicit` ahead of the word class. An implicit class follows the same rules of every other class. The `implicit` makes the class the primary constructor available when we require an implicit conversion with the class in the scope. An implicit class can be defined only inside an object, trait, or class.

GraphicHelper defines a class UpdateCanvas. This is used to override the canvas of the game. We can see in all game engines elements that are designed to be used for other parts of the engine. The UpdateCanvas class is designed to be used in different kinds of graphics contexts, for example, to draw the graphics in an Android app or in a AWT graphics interface. In our case, the important part of the code is the name we give to the method. We must always remember that the DSL is not just a technique for programming but, most important, is the name we use to define the method and the variables inside the software.

GraphicHelper defines some other classes inside it, such as the Animation class. This is used to manage the animation during the game.

```
class Animation(
  var frameDuration: Long,
  frames: Array[ImageRegion],
  var playMode: Animation.PlayMode = Animation.Normal
)
{
  def currentFrame(time: Long): ImageRegion = {
    val frameNumber: Int = ((time/frameDuration) % Int.
    MaxValue).toInt

    val frameIndex = playMode match {
      case Animation.Normal =>
        math.min(frames.size - 1, frameNumber)
      case Animation.Reversed =>
        math.max(frames.size - frameNumber - 1, 0)
      case Animation.Loop =>
        frameNumber % frames.size
      case Animation.LoopReversed =>
        frames.length - (frameNumber % frames.size) - 1
    }

    frames(frameIndex)
  }

  def IsCompleted(time: Long): Boolean = time > animation
  Duration

  def Duration: Long = frames.size*frameDuration
}
```

The class has two methods. `currentFrame` is used to define the frame index of the animation. An animation is nothing more than a set of frames, one following the other within a short time. We can define different kinds of animation. These are identified by `playMode`. The calculation of the frame is achieved by using the math library. We define the minimum and the maximum for every frame.

The code of the class is a little bit complex. First, we define the kind of animation we want to create. This is done when we create the class, and we send the following parameters:

```
var frameDuration: Long,
frames: Array[ImageRegion],
var playMode: Animation.PlayMode = Animation.Normal
```

These parameters are used to initialize the class. Now, we can see defined the values used to define the animation. An animation is a set of *frames*. A frame is a single image. We can define the velocity of the animation, meaning how many frames per second we must have to realize the animation. The normal speed of an animation is 24 fps (frames per second). Tree parameters are used to define this value. Usually, the frame is designed in what we call *sprite sheets*. This file contains a set of images of the animation we want to create. Every image has a dimension, and this dimension is used to calculate how many frames are present in the animation. `ImageRegion` essentially defines the "area" of the frame.

This utility class is used by the graphic component.

```
package ch10

import util.Loader

trait GraphicsSystem extends GraphicHelper {
  this: SystemProvider =>

  trait Graphics {
```

```
  def loadImage(path: System.ResourcePath): Loader[Bitmap]

}
val Graphics: Graphics

//Define and abstract class Bitmap, this is used for define the
size of the image we need to use
abstract class AbstractBitmap {
  def height: Int
  def width: Int
}
type Bitmap <: AbstractBitmap

  def loadImageFromResource(path: String): Bitmap

//This class is used to define the type of Font we want to
create
abstract class AbstractFont {

  def withSize(size: Int): Font
  def withStyle(style: Font.Style): Font

  def isBold(): Boolean
  def isItalic(): Boolean

}

type Font <: AbstractFont

abstract class FontCompanion {
  def create(family: String, style: Style, size: Int): Font

  val Default: Font
  val DefaultBold: Font
  val Monospace: Font
  val SansSerif: Font
  val Serif: Font
```

```
    sealed trait Style
    case object Bold extends Style
    case object BoldItalic extends Style
    case object Italic extends Style
    case object Normal extends Style
    }
  val Font: FontCompanion

  type Color
  //Define the abstract to define the different kinds of colors
  abstract class ColorCompanion {

    def rgb(r: Int, g: Int, b: Int): Color

    def rgba(r: Int, g: Int, b: Int, a: Int): Color

    def Black: Color = rgb(0, 0, 0)
    def Blue: Color = rgb(0, 0, 255)
    def Cyan: Color = rgb(0, 255, 255)
    def DarkGray: Color = rgb(68, 68, 68)
    def Gray: Color = rgb(136, 136, 136)
    def Green: Color = rgb(0, 255, 0)
    def LightGray: Color = rgb(204, 204, 204)
    def Magenta: Color = rgb(255, 0, 255)
    def Red: Color = rgb(255, 0, 0)
    def White: Color = rgb(255, 255, 255)
    def Yellow: Color = rgb(255, 255, 0)
  }
  val Color: ColorCompanion

//Define the alignment for the text and the element
 object Alignments {
    sealed trait Alignment
    case object Center extends Alignment
```

```scala
  case object Left extends Alignment
  case object Right extends Alignment
}
//Define how to draw the font, with what color and what
alignments
trait AbstractPaint {
  def font: Font
  def withFont(font: Font): Paint

  def color: Color
  def withColor(color: Color): Paint

  def alignment: Alignments.Alignment
  def withAlignment(alignment: Alignments.Alignment): Paint
}

type Paint <: AbstractPaint
def defaultPaint: Paint

trait AbstractTextLayout {
  def height: Int
}
type TextLayout <: AbstractTextLayout
//Define the graphic elements for the interface
trait AbstractCanvas {

  def width: Int
  def height: Int

  def withSave[A](body: => A): A
  def translate(x: Int, y: Int): Unit

  def rotate(theta: Double): Unit

  def scale(sx: Double, sy: Double): Unit
```

```
  def clipRect(x: Int, y: Int, width: Int, height: Int): Unit

  def drawBitmap(bitmap: Bitmap, x: Int, y: Int): Unit

  def drawBitmap(bitmap: Bitmap, dx: Int, dy: Int, sx: Int,
  sy: Int, width: Int, height: Int): Unit

  def drawRect(x: Int, y: Int, width: Int, height: Int,
  paint: Paint): Unit

  def drawOval(x: Int, y: Int, width: Int, height: Int,
  paint: Paint): Unit
  def drawLine(x1: Int, y1: Int, x2: Int, y2: Int, paint:
  Paint): Unit

  def drawCircle(x: Int, y: Int, radius: Int, paint: Paint):
  Unit = drawOval(x, y, 2*radius, 2*radius, paint)

  def drawString(str: String, x: Int, y: Int, paint: Paint):
  Unit
  def drawText(text: TextLayout, x: Int, y: Int): Unit

  def drawColor(color: Color): Unit

  def clearRect(x: Int, y: Int, width: Int, height: Int):
  Unit
  def clear(): Unit = clearRect(0, 0, width, height)

  def renderText(text: String, width: Int, paint: Paint):
  TextLayout
 }
 type Canvas <: AbstractCanvas

 def getScreenCanvas: Canvas
 def releaseScreenCanvas(canvas: Canvas): Unit

}
```

Now we can see how the GraphicsSystem uses the GraphicHelper. What it does is define all methods for drawing primitives on the screen. In this case, we define the method as in English. This helps when we need to use that.

This code sometimes requires explanation and is what we do now. The class first defines GraphicsSystem. This is an extension of the GraphicHelper trait. As we've seen, a trait is similar to a Java interface. The code we use follows:

```
trait Graphics {

  def loadImage(path: System.ResourcePath): Loader[Bitmap]

}
```

This trait defines the method loadImage. Now, the method indicates that we load an image from a path. This is basic to every game engine.

Now, the engine must have the size of the image to calculate the duration of the animation. For this reason, we create an abstract class called AbstractBitmap. This class has two methods to define the dimension of the bitmap: height and length. These are used to identify the bitmap exactly.

Something else we must define for the graphics is the font. To do this, we create another abstract class to define the kind of font we use. The class is AbstractFont. Now, we can define all typographic necessary for the font.

In the class, we define all the graphic components we require to create the graphics. The note of this class is the AbstractCanvas trait. This trait is essentially the core of the software. We use this trait to define every type of image we want to draw. For example, we define the circle, the rectangle, etc. All these elements are used to define that of the user interface. One note is the use of *type*. Type in Scala is used to create an alias for some complex piece of code. In our case, we use a type to connect to some different kind of class.

Other Components

So far, we have defined the components for graphics, but in a game engine, we must define other components to control the game. This class de facto intercepts the key of the keyboard, or the mouse, and responds to a specific event, as follows:

```
package ch10

trait InputHelper extends StateMachine {
  this: Input =>
  //The input helper is used for define all the input method
  defined in the game in this class we define every type of input
  we can use in the game for example the keyboard and the mouse
  object InputHelper {

    import Input._
    //This is used to define the "event" the event is used to
    define what's happening on the game, it is similar to the
    event in normal graphic development, there is a poll, a set
    of events, the software must be able to process every event
    and reply with the correct functionality to the event
    def pollEvent(): Option[InputEvent] = {
      val ev = Input.pollEvent()
      ev foreach processEvent
      ev
    }
    def processEvents(function: (InputEvent) => Unit): Unit = {
      var oev = Input.pollEvent()
      while(!oev.isEmpty) {
        val ev = oev.get
        processEvent(ev)
        function(ev)
```

```
  oev = pollEvent()
 }
}
//the method processEvent is used to identify the event,
this method essentially checks what event is raised and
then creates the class to respond to the event itself
def processEvent(event: InputEvent): Unit = event match {
  case KeyDownEvent(key) => setKeyboardState(key, true)
  case KeyUpEvent(key) => setKeyboardState(key, false)
  case MouseMovedEvent(x, y) => Inputs.Mouse.position =
  (x, y)
  case MouseDownEvent(x, y, mouseButton) => {
    Inputs.Mouse.position = (x, y)
    mouseButton match {
      case Input.MouseButtons.Left =>
        Inputs.Buttons.leftPressed = true
      case Input.MouseButtons.Right =>
        Inputs.Buttons.rightPressed = true
      case Input.MouseButtons.Middle =>
        Inputs.Buttons.middlePressed = true
    }
  }
  case MouseUpEvent(x, y, mouseButton) => {
    Inputs.Mouse.position = (x, y)
    mouseButton match {
      case Input.MouseButtons.Left =>
        Inputs.Buttons.leftPressed = false
      case Input.MouseButtons.Right =>
        Inputs.Buttons.rightPressed = false
      case Input.MouseButtons.Middle =>
        Inputs.Buttons.middlePressed = false
    }
  }
```

```
    }
    case MouseScrolledEvent(amount) => ()
    case TouchMovedEvent(x, y, pointer) => (
      Inputs.Touch.pointerPressed += (pointer -> (x, y))
    )
    case TouchDownEvent(x, y, pointer) => (
      Inputs.Touch.pointerPressed += (pointer -> (x, y))
    )
    case TouchUpEvent(x, y, pointer) => (
      Inputs.Touch.pointerPressed -= pointer
    )
  }
  //This method is used to define the input state of the
  keyboard, when we press a key, essentially we change the
  state of the key we press, this class is used to intercept
  that and then change the state. The change of state is used
  to create the response on the game
  private def setKeyboardState(key: Input.Keys.Key, down:
  Boolean): Unit = key match {
    case Keys.Left => Inputs.Keyboard.left = down
    case Keys.Up => Inputs.Keyboard.up = down
    case Keys.Right => Inputs.Keyboard.right = down
    case Keys.Down => Inputs.Keyboard.down = down

    case Keys.Space => Inputs.Keyboard.space = down

    case Keys.ButtonStart => Inputs.Buttons.startPressed
    = down
    case Keys.ButtonSelect => Inputs.Buttons.selectPressed
    = down

    case Keys.ButtonBack => Inputs.Buttons.backPressed = down
    case Keys.ButtonMenu => Inputs.Buttons.menuPressed = down
```

```
case Keys.A => Inputs.Keyboard.a = down
case Keys.B => Inputs.Keyboard.b = down
case Keys.C => Inputs.Keyboard.c = down
case Keys.D => Inputs.Keyboard.d = down
case Keys.E => Inputs.Keyboard.e = down
case Keys.F => Inputs.Keyboard.f = down
case Keys.G => Inputs.Keyboard.g = down
case Keys.H => Inputs.Keyboard.h = down
case Keys.I => Inputs.Keyboard.i = down
case Keys.J => Inputs.Keyboard.j = down
case Keys.K => Inputs.Keyboard.k = down
case Keys.L => Inputs.Keyboard.l = down
case Keys.M => Inputs.Keyboard.m = down
case Keys.N => Inputs.Keyboard.n = down
case Keys.O => Inputs.Keyboard.o = down
case Keys.P => Inputs.Keyboard.p = down
case Keys.Q => Inputs.Keyboard.q = down
case Keys.R => Inputs.Keyboard.r = down
case Keys.S => Inputs.Keyboard.s = down
case Keys.T => Inputs.Keyboard.t = down
case Keys.U => Inputs.Keyboard.u = down
case Keys.V => Inputs.Keyboard.v = down
case Keys.W => Inputs.Keyboard.w = down
case Keys.X => Inputs.Keyboard.x = down
case Keys.Y => Inputs.Keyboard.y = down
case Keys.Z => Inputs.Keyboard.z = down

case Keys.Num0 => Inputs.Keyboard.num0 = down
case Keys.Num1 => Inputs.Keyboard.num1 = down
case Keys.Num2 => Inputs.Keyboard.num2 = down
case Keys.Num3 => Inputs.Keyboard.num3 = down
case Keys.Num4 => Inputs.Keyboard.num4 = down
```

```scala
      case Keys.Num5 => Inputs.Keyboard.num5 = down
      case Keys.Num6 => Inputs.Keyboard.num6 = down
      case Keys.Num7 => Inputs.Keyboard.num7 = down
      case Keys.Num8 => Inputs.Keyboard.num8 = down
      case Keys.Num9 => Inputs.Keyboard.num9 = down
    }

  }
//The object input is used to define the input for the game, the
input can be sent by the keyboard or by a mouse
  object Input {

    object ButtonPressed {
      var left: Boolean = false
      var middle: Boolean = false
      var right: Boolean = false
      var back: Boolean = false
      var menu: Boolean = false
      var start: Boolean = false
      var select: Boolean = false
    }
    //This defines the object touch, this is used to identify
    where the player points and touches during the game
    object Touch {
      var pointerPressed: Map[Int, (Int, Int)] = Map()

      def pressed: Option[(Int, Int)] = pointerPressed.toSeq.
      headOption.map(_._2)
      def pressed(pointer: Int): Option[(Int, Int)] =
      pointerPressed.get(pointer)

      def allPressed: Seq[(Int, (Int, Int))] = pointerPressed.
      toSeq
    }
```

```
//The object Mouse is used to identify and describe the
mouse, every game actually uses a mouse for play and then
our engine needs one object
object Mouse {
  var position: (Int, Int) = (0, 0)

  def pressed: Option[(Int, Int)] = leftPressed
  def leftPressed: Option[(Int, Int)] = if(Buttons.
  leftPressed) Some(position) else None
  def rightPressed: Option[(Int, Int)] = if(Buttons.
  rightPressed) Some(position) else None
}
```

```
//This object simulates the keyboard, what we do there is
essentially re-create all layouts for the keyboard
//we define the key with a boolean, this is used to define if the
key is pressed or not
object Keyboard {
    var left: Boolean = false
    var right: Boolean = false
    var up: Boolean = false
    var down: Boolean = false

    var space: Boolean = false

    var a: Boolean = false
    var b: Boolean = false
    var c: Boolean = false
    var d: Boolean = false
    var e: Boolean = false
    var f: Boolean = false
    var g: Boolean = false
    var h: Boolean = false
    var i: Boolean = false
```

```
    var j: Boolean = false
    var k: Boolean = false
    var l: Boolean = false
    var m: Boolean = false
    var n: Boolean = false
    var o: Boolean = false
    var p: Boolean = false
    var q: Boolean = false
    var r: Boolean = false
    var s: Boolean = false
    var t: Boolean = false
    var u: Boolean = false
    var v: Boolean = false
    var w: Boolean = false
    var x: Boolean = false
    var y: Boolean = false
    var z: Boolean = false

    var num0: Boolean = false
    var num1: Boolean = false
    var num2: Boolean = false
    var num3: Boolean = false
    var num4: Boolean = false
    var num5: Boolean = false
    var num6: Boolean = false
    var num7: Boolean = false
    var num8: Boolean = false
    var num9: Boolean = false
}
//This class is used to identify the usage of the mouse,
now we can see we use the object Mouse, this object tells
to      //the programm what key is pressed
```

```
object PointDevice {
  def pressed: Option[(Int, Int)] = Mouse.leftPressed.
  orElse(Touch.pressed)
}

}
}
```

This method defines all events we can use to define all keys and events raised in the game. This allows the engine to respond to the keys pressed or to the mouse's click. This class is simple and another example of a key principle of DSLs: defined methods can be read like plain English.

Conclusion

So far, you have seen DSL used in different fields. The last I discussed is the video game. In this chapter, I have highlighted how a DSL can be used in everyday development, not only to define a specific pattern or use a specific technique, but, for example, to define a name for a method and variable that can be used in plain English. The DSL can be integrated in everyday development, starting with simple steps. The most important change we can make with the DSL is to begin to think about the method and the variable in plain English. After that, we can start to improve the method and the pattern involved in that.

CHAPTER 11

Cloud and DevOps

Cloud and DevOps are currently the hot tickets for many organizations.
Increasingly, businesses are migrating to the cloud and adopting DevOps
to meet their everyday requirements.

DevOps helps organizations to reduce the time to market of their
products and/or services, and cloud computing helps to reduce
infrastructure costs. By freeing a business from having to maintain its
own servers, and by helping to solve problems faster, costs are reduced.
For example, if there is a problem with a server, if it is in the cloud, a
new server can be created, instead of spending resources to repair the
broken one.

In particular, DevOps and cloud are used for microservices, as
discussed in Chapter 5. In this chapter, I introduce some DevOps practices
and describe how to use Scala and DSLs to create and deploy services in
the cloud.

What Is DevOps?

DevOps is a portmanteau word formed from the union of "dev," for
developer, and "ops," for *operational*. These two words encompass the
entire software life cycle and represent a set of practices born of the idea
of removing every friction during the development life cycle. The growth
of DevOps coincided with that of the cloud. It is not unusual to see cloud
companies adopt DevOps for managing their development life cycles.

© Pierluigi Riti 2018
P. Riti, *Practical Scala DSLs*, https://doi.org/10.1007/978-1-4842-3036-7_11

DevOps was described as "on the rise" by Gartner in 2013. That description was characterizing what was then an emerging technology. In the last four years, DevOps has become the latest sensation at many companies.

If we wanted to define DevOps, we could say that it is a set of practices across a company, with the goal of reducing the time to market of every initiative and improving the quality of the product releases.

This simple definition is at the core of DevOps.

- *Quality*: The goal of DevOps is to improve and guarantee the quality of the software in every single deployment. This is done to put in practice some common procedures during development and deployment.

- *Reduce the time to market*: It is important to reduce the time from the release of the code in the repo to the final build. To do that, DevOps adopts continuous integration (CI). Every component of the code is built and tested immediately.

- *Improve the communication across the company*: The purpose of DevOps is to reduce friction across the company. To accomplish that, it shares common practices company-wide.

Of course, the successful adoption of DevOps requires some common practices. These help to introduce them across the company and ensure the success of their implementation.

Common DevOps Practice

To be successful, DevOps introduces some practices that help make operations smoother and more efficient. These practices can be summarized as follows:

- Ops professionals should be the leading citizens of the software architecture. They are the people responsible for maintaining the code. Involving them in the design of the architecture helps to create better logs, and this translates into less downgrade time in case of error.

- Developers should be responsible for breaking the code in production. Usually, after developers complete a job, their involvement ends. This creates a mentality by which the developer doesn't really care about what happens in production. Allowing developers to be responsible when there is a problem in production has two significant benefits. First, the developer can help to fix the issue faster, and second, the developer is able to know what happens when the code is broken.

- The company should ensure that all its employees use the same build process. Having a clear build and deployment process across the company helps to improve quality and reduce time to market.

- Continuous deployment (CD)and CI should be adopted for a better build process and better release. Both practices ensure a smoother and faster build. These processes involve only the new part of the code and not all the code, which reduces build time and helps to identify errors more quickly.

- The infrastructure-as-code design should be
  implemented, which ensures better and more reliable
  infrastructure, particularly in the cloud.

All these practices should be taken together to help to initiate good
DevOps procedures and reduce the time to market. They should be
approved and sponsored by management. It is important for management
to understand the value of these procedures and help to put them in place
in the correct manner. DevOps is important for every company to be
successful in business right now.

At this point, what we want to do is begin to create some code that can
be used to design our infrastructure. The software we use to do this is Scala
and AWS. These will support the CI and CD in every project. Of course,
we must have some basic methodologies that allow, in particular, test-
driven development (TDD). With this kind of software development, using
XP programming, a developer writes the test for the code first. The test is
based on user input, and then the code for passing the test is written. This
is basically what takes place in the practice of CI and CD.

Start with AWS

The first step in AWS development is to create a free AWS account.
To create a free one-year account, go to https://aws.amazon.com/.
Remember: You must enter a valid credit card credential to begin the trial.
When you have logged in to the new account, you will see something like
Figure 11-1.

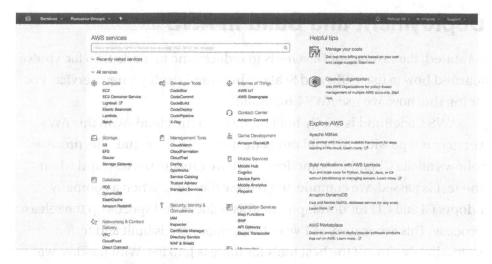

Figure 11-1. *The AWS console*

We can see that a lot of different services are at our disposal. What we want to concentrate on in this chapter is EC2 and Lambda.

To begin to develop, we must install an SDK. Unfortunately, Amazon doesn't produce an SDK for Scala, but we can use the Java version, so the next step is to install the SDK from Java. To download the SDK, go to https://aws.amazon.com/sdk-for-java/ install and try via the console to see if the SDK has been correctly installed. For this, just write aws in the console. If all is working correctly, you will see something like Figure 11-2.

```
usage: aws [options] <command> <subcommand> [<subcommand> ...] [parameters]
To see help text, you can run:

  aws help
  aws <command> help
  aws <command> <subcommand> help
aws: error: too few arguments
```

Figure 11-2. *The AWS command line interface*

This shows that the AWS is installed. Now we can start to write our code.

Deployment and Build in AWS

As stated, the essence of DevOps is to reduce time to market. So far, you've learned how to use DSLs and Scala to build and deploy a new service. For doing that now, we use AWS CodeBuild.

AWS CodeBuild is a fully built manager in the cloud. With this AWS service, it is possible to build our code directly in the cloud. The process follows all the CI and CD practices. First, we execute the test, and when the test is passed, we compile and release the code. When a company adopts CI and CD for development, this reduces and speeds up the release process. This is because, as I've noted, component is built and tested immediately. One of the best tools for these is Jenkins. With Jenkins, we can create a set build that allows us to run and check the status of every single build. Every build is made at the same time we release the code, and this helps us to uncover any errors at the time of the build.

The service is very useful when we have to create a microservice and release it in a fast and reliable way. Now, what we want to do is prepare some code and see how to use DSL techniques for this.

Because we are executing the code for the cloud, I suggest using a docker image for sbt. This is because it is easy to set up and use. Following is the command to download the docker image I used:

```
docker pull hseeberger/scala-sbt
```

This has all we need to start our project.

With the image downloaded, we can start to write some code. In our case, the directory structure is very important. The final directory will be like Figure 11-3.

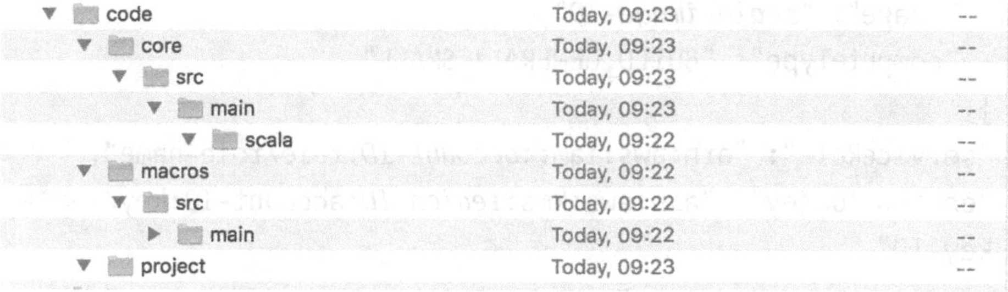

▼ 📁 code	Today, 09:23	--
▼ 📁 core	Today, 09:23	--
▼ 📁 src	Today, 09:23	--
▼ 📁 main	Today, 09:23	--
▼ 📁 scala	Today, 09:22	--
▼ 📁 macros	Today, 09:22	--
▼ 📁 src	Today, 09:22	--
▶ 📁 main	Today, 09:22	--
▼ 📁 project	Today, 09:23	--

Figure 11-3. *AWS Scala macro package structure*

This is the structure we use for our first sample code. Now, it is time to start to write some code.

Creating the Project in AWS

First, to create the AWS for the project, we must use the AWS CLI. The code for this follows:

```
{
  "name": "chapt_11_practicalscala",
  "source": {
    "type": "S3",
    "location": "codebuild-region-ID-account-ID-input-bucket/
    PracticalScalaDSL.zip"
  },
  "artifacts": {
    "type": "S3",
    "location": "codebuild-region-ID-account-ID-output-bucket",
    "packaging": "ZIP",
    "name": "PracticalScalaDSLOutput.zip"
  },
  "environment": {
    "type": "LINUX_CONTAINER",
```

```
  "image": "scala-image-ID",
  "computeType": "BUILD_GENERAL1_SMALL"
},
"serviceRole": "arn:aws:iam::account-ID:role/role-name",
"encryptionKey": "arn:aws:kms:region-ID:account-ID:key/
key-ID"
}
```

The code can be executed using the following command:

```
aws create-project aws_project.json
```

This creates in our AWS instance the structure of the code.

Note   In the code, some data should be added by the user, particularly the account-id and the region-id. All this data can be received when the user creates his or her own AWS account.

This code creates the basic artifact for our code. Now, we can start to create the other file necessary for our project.

Creating the Basic Files

The first file we create is buildspec.yml. This file is used to define all the commands we use to build our software. For example, we may have a file such as the following:

```
version: 0.2

phases:
  build:
    commands:
      - echo Build started on `date`
```

```
      - echo Run the test and package the code...
      - sbt run
  post_build:
    commands:
      - echo Build completed on `date`
      - sbt package
artifacts:
  files:
    - core/target/scala-2.11/core_2.11-1.0.0.jar
```

We can see that this file uses a DSL, a specific language for defining every state of the build. This file is used to build our project. You can see that we are using the sbt command to build our Scala project.

In DevOps, it is necessary to write tests, so the next file we create is a simple test file.

```scala
object PracticalScalaDSLTest extends App {
  PracticalScalaDSL.sayHello
}
```

This code is very simple and calls the method sayHello from another object. This Scala file is what we execute when we build our code.

What we want now is to write the code to pass the test. The code for that is

```scala
import scala.language.experimental.macros
import scala.reflect.macros.Context

object PracticalScalaDSL {
  def impl(c: Context) = {
    import c.universe._
    c.Expr[Unit](q"""println("Hello Scala AWS")""")
  }

  def sayHello: Unit = macro impl
}
```

This code uses Scala macros. Macros, a new way to define code, were introduced in Scala version 2.10 and are very useful for defining DSL code. Macros are essentially a function called by the compiler during the compilation. In our case, the function impl is called and created during the compilation. This is another use for the DSL. We can define different functions and don't use them until we compile. This technique is called *metaprogramming*.

You've now seen how to call the macro in the function sayHello. The line macro impl essentially calls the execution of our macro. The function doesn't know what the macro does, only to take care to call the implementation of the macro. This can be used to define different functions in different contexts, and this flexibility is the essence of DSLs.

Creating the Build File

What we must do now is create the Scala build file for the project. The file is

```
import sbt._
import Keys._

object BuildSettings {
  val buildSettings = Defaults.defaultSettings ++ Seq(
    organization := "practical.scaladsl",
    version := "1.0.0",
    scalaVersion := "2.11.8",
    crossScalaVersions := Seq("2.10.2", "2.10.3", "2.10.4",
    "2.10.5", "2.10.6", "2.11.0", "2.11.1", "2.11.2", "2.11.3",
    "2.11.4", "2.11.5", "2.11.6", "2.11.7", "2.11.8"),
    resolvers += Resolver.sonatypeRepo("snapshots"),
    resolvers += Resolver.sonatypeRepo("releases"),
    scalacOptions ++= Seq()
  )
}
```

```scala
object PracticalScalaDSLBuuld extends Build {
  import BuildSettings._

  lazy val root: Project = Project(
    "root",
    file("."),
    settings = buildSettings ++ Seq(
      run <<= run in Compile in core)
  ) aggregate(macros, core)

  lazy val macros: Project = Project(
    "macros",
    file("practicalscaladsl"),
    settings = buildSettings ++ Seq(
      libraryDependencies <+= (scalaVersion)("org.scala-lang" %
      "scala-reflect" % _),
      libraryDependencies := {
        CrossVersion.partialVersion(scalaVersion.value) match {
          // if Scala 2.11+ is used, quasiquotes are available
          in the standard distribution
          case Some((2, scalaMajor)) if scalaMajor >= 11 =>
            libraryDependencies.value
          // in Scala 2.10, quasiquotes are provided by macro
          paradise
          case Some((2, 10)) =>
            libraryDependencies.value ++ Seq(
              compilerPlugin("org.scalamacros" % "paradise" %
              "2.1.0-M5" cross CrossVersion.full),
              "org.scalamacros" %% "quasiquotes" % "2.1.0-M5"
              cross CrossVersion.binary)
        }
      }
```

```
    )
  )

  lazy val core: Project = Project(
    "core",
    file("core"),
    settings = buildSettings
  ) dependsOn(macros)
}
```

This code essentially creates our build process and defines all we need to install our service in the cloud. The code is essentially a big DSL specific to the build.

Final Conclusion

You have seen how to create and use DSLs across different platforms and requirements. This chapter showed how to build software made in the cloud. This can be used in tandem with the microservice to deploy our architecture and release it in the cloud. I defined some DevOps practices and showed, as well, how these can be used with a DSL. This concludes our journey, and I hope you have enjoyed it.

Now you understand that DSLs are not only a programming technique but, essentially, a way of developing better code.

Index

A

AbstractBitmap, 199
Abstract syntax tree (AST)
    pattern, 116
    heterogeneous, 119
    homogenous, 116–119
    irregular heterogeneous, 119
    normalized heterogeneous, 118
Account type, 165
Android Studio, 140–142, 147
Application program interface
    (API), 30–32, 39–40
    _account_value, 173
    import, 172
    package, 170–171
    rules and experience, 167–168
AWS
    command line interface, 213
    project creation, 215–216
    Scala macro package, 214–215

B

Backus-Naus Form (BNF), 98–99
    definition, 60
    rules, 63
    syntactic analysis, 62

C

Comma-separated values (CSV), 30
Conditional expression, 16
Continuous integration (CI),
    34–35, 41
Conway's Law, 75
CurrencyPair class, 163–164

D

Data structure
    array, 24–25
    list, 24–26
    map, 24, 27
    set, 24, 26
    tuple, 24, 26–27
Delimiter-direct transaction, 63
DevOps
    definition, 210
    practices, 211–212
    Scala build file, 218–220
Domain problem
    EBNF, 104
    grammar, 104
    JSON parser, 108, 110–111
    parser preparation, 105–106
    rules

Get the eBook for only $5!

Why limit yourself?

With most of our titles available in both PDF and ePUB format, you can access your content wherever and however you wish—on your PC, phone, tablet, or reader.

Since you've purchased this print book, we are happy to offer you the eBook for just $5.

To learn more, go to http://www.apress.com/companion or contact support@apress.com.

Apress®

Printed in the United States
By Bookmasters